CORPUS PALLADIANUM

VOLUME VII

CENTRO INTERNAZIONALE DI STUDI DI ARCHITETTURA
" ANDREA PALLADIO "

CORPUS PALLADIANUM

Editor of the Series: Renato Cevese

Assistant Editor: Abelardo Cappelletti

THE VILLA BADOER
AT FRATTA POLESINE

Lionello Puppi

THE VILLA BADOER
AT FRATTA POLESINE

Translated by Catherine Enggass

CORPUS PALLADIANUM

VOLUME VII

THE PENNSYLVANIA STATE UNIVERSITY PRESS
UNIVERSITY PARK & LONDON

I AM MOST GRATEFUL TO THE CENTRO INTERNAZIONALE DI STUDI DI ARCHI-
TETTURA « A. PALLADIO » OF VICENZA FOR THE OPPORTUNITY GIVEN ME TO
DO THIS STUDY. I WISH ESPECIALLY TO EXPRESS MY GRATITUDE TO PROF.
RODOLFO PALLUCCHINI, PROF. RENATO CEVESE, ARCH. ANDREA PERESWET-
SOLTAN AND DOTT. FERNANDO RIGON FOR THEIR CONTINUOUS INTEREST
IN THIS WORK. I AM OBLIGED TO PROF. WOLFANG LOTZ AND PARTICULARLY
TO PROF. ERIK FORSSMAN FOR THEIR USEFUL SUGGESTIONS. FOR THE COURTESY
WITH WHICH THEY HAVE ASSISTED ME IN EVERY WAY I WISH TO EXPRESS
MY THANKS TO ON. PROF. GUIUSEPPE ROMANATO, PRESIDENT OF THE ACCADE-
MIA DEI CONCORDI OF ROVIGO; DOTT. GIANLUIGI CERUTI AND SIGNOR
SERGIO GUERRA; DOTT. LINO BOSCHETTO OF THE STATE ARCHIVES OF
VENICE; PROF. TERISIO PIGNATTI, DIRECTOR OF THE CORRER MUSEUM, AND
DOTT. LUCIA CASANOVA, DIRECTOR OF THE CORRER LIBRARY OF VENICE;
DOTT. GIORGIO E. FERRARI, DIRECTOR OF THE MARCIANA LIBRARY OF
VENICE; DOTT. GINO BENZONI OF THE ISTITUTO PER LA STORIA DELLA
SOCIETÁ E DELLO STATO VENEZIANO OF THE G. CINI FOUNDATION OF VE-
NICE (THE SAME VALUABLE ASSISTANCE WAS GIVEN TO ME IN THE OTHER
VENETIAN INSTITUTES, AND I WISH TO EXPRESS MY GRATITUDE TO PROF.
ALESSANDRO BETTAGNO, DOTT. MARIA TERESA MURARO, AND SIGNOR AL-
FREDO TACCO); COMM. ARMANDO LICONTI OF THE ARCHIVIO NOTARILE
DISTRETTUALE OF ROVIGO; DOTT. BRUNO RIGOBELLO, DIRECTOR OF THE
CONSORZIO DI BONIFICA VALDENTRO-VESPARA E PRESE UNITE DI LENDINARA;
DON BRUNO SEGALA, PARISH PRIEST OF FRATTA POLESINE; AND SIGNOR
SANTO DOLCETTO, CARETAKER OF VILLA BADOER.

SOMMARIO

THE VILLA BADOER AT FRATTA POLESINE

LIST OF ABBREVIATIONS

ACL   =   Archivio del Consorzio di Bonifica Valdentro-Vespara e Prese Unite di Lendinara
ACR   =   Archivio Storico del Comune di Rovigo
ANR   =   Archivio Notarile Distrettuale di Rovigo
APF   =   Archivio Parrocchiale di Fratta Polesine
ASMa =   Archivio di Stato di Mantova
ASMo =   Archivio di Stato di Modena
ASV   =   Archivio di Stato di Venezia
BCR   =   Biblioteca dei Concordi di Rovigo
BCV   =   Biblioteca Civica Correr di Venezia
BMV   =   Biblioteca Nazionale Marciana di Venezia
CISA =   Centro Internazionale di Studi di Architettura "A. Palladio" di Vicenza
ÖNB   =   Österreichische National Bibliothek, Vienna
RIBA =   Royal Institute of British Architects, London

a. - Frontal view of Villa Badoer

I
PATRONAGE

The origins of the series of events that led to the commission for the construction of Villa Badoer at Fratta Polesine have deep roots. In both their subjective and objective aspects they are inextricably linked to the effects of a singular friendship, later to be solidified and heightened by the ties of kinship. We know through a statement by Vasari, reinforced and sanctioned by Palladio himself, that the promotor of the work was the "magnificent Signor Francesco Badoer,"[1] a member of one of the less prestigious branches of the illustrious Venetian family. The work of the genealogists—utilized by the scholars most closely concerned with problems of patronage, such as Burger and, even more zealously, Zorzi[2]—offers essential information regarding this personage. They sketch a modest figure whose public career was devoid of outstanding episodes. Born the son of Piero di Albertino on September 5, 1512, he was, it appears, the second of five brothers—the others being Angelo, Andrea, Albertino, and Giovanni Luigi.[3] Francesco was a member of the Council and a Senator and in 1562 served as *Capitano* in Bergamo.[4] In 1536 he married Lucietta, the daughter of Giovanfrancesco Loredan.[5] (The abundant implications and consequences of the marriage will be discussed later.) From this marriage came four sons, Giovanni, Andrea, Marcantonio, and Piero, and two daughters.[6]

The death of Francesco Badoer very probably took place in 1572.[7] Archival documents confirm that after Cambrai, which was a turning point, the Badoers followed the political-economic tendencies of the Venetian aristocracy, employing the financial capital produced by previous mercantile activities in investments in land to guarantee slower but more secure profits. If not an exclusive choice, it was an explicit and irreversible one. We know in particular that they turned their attention to land within Venice and in Padua.[8] Indeed, in the declaration presented by Piero di Albertino Badoer to the fiscal authority for the *Estimo* (the Land Valuation Office) in 1537, his real estate holdings located in Camposampiero, Mirano, etc., are recorded. Piero died in 1548.[9] On May 21, 1550, at the time of the division of his estate among the living sons, Andrea, Francesco, and Angelo, there is no mention of any investments in Polesine.[10] In principle, such a confirmation should not be surprising; the Badoers's commitment to the land reflects a characteristic and widespread orientation typical of the first phase of the so-called *rentière* speculation on the part of the Venetian nobles. On the one hand, this orientation is deprecatingly and tendentiously indicated by Priuli in his statement, "And yet there was no citizen or noble, or common man, who having the means had not at least bought property and a house in Terrafirma, and especially in the area of Padua and Treviso in order to have a place nearby to go for diversion and to return in one or two days." On the other hand, a considerable number of transactions of this kind are documented.[11] Francesco Badoer's unexpected and almost inexplicable change of course in investment, astonishing in its dimensions, is verified by a declaration to the *Estimo*: "in Polesine de Rovigo ... 460 acres," "in the Vespara ... a piece of land called the Valle di Santa Maria ... in the aforesaid area of Vespara" held "in common with the Magnificent Signor Vincenzo Grimani son of the Magnificent Signor Antonio," "about seven acres ... in Villa della Fratta in a place called Bragola," "ten acres... in Villa de la Costa."[12] Actually, the provenance of the "seven acres" in Fratta is specified: they "were bought from the government" (or, in the phrase that is used regularly, from *li signori sopra le camere*).[13] It thus seems reasonable to suspect that he procured the land at a bargain. This suspicion is proved by a decisive document of 1545 which not only clarifies the otherwise incomprehensible reasons for Grimani's "presence" but, above all, opens wider and more meaningful considerations. Appearing before the Venetian notary Bonifacio Soliano quondam Matteo on December 14, 1545, the brothers Girolamo and Giovanni Cornaro, acting on their own behalf, and Francesco Badoer and Vincenzo Grimani, acting on behalf of the sisters of the deceased Giorgio Loredan, proprietors "in common ... of the forest and the holdings of Vespara" (each side with one-half share), had the land surveyed and divided and requested that the division be effectuated. In this manner the Loredan heirs received one section of 1,112 acres and the Cornaro heirs the other section of 1,193 acres.[14]

The text requires some clarification. The Venetian Senate needed to raise funds for the state, above all for the State Bank which had been compromised by the expenses sustained in the recent wars and further weakened by the financial burdens imposed by the terms of the truce concluded with the Imperial forces on July 31, 1518. Consequently, on February 25, 1518 (1519—Venetian reckoning) the Senate decided to "sell at a public auction all the possessions and other properties of the Signoria of any sort, situated in the Polesine di Rovigo,"[15] properties acquired, as is known, from the Dukes of Ferrara.[16] A little later we note that "all the holdings in Vespara," which comprised 2,000 acres (using the Paduan measure) were put up for auction. On July 13, 1519, we finally learn that "factis pluribus incontris, [... the property] deliberata fuit Joanni Francisco Lauredano quondam Marci Antonii et sociis."[17] It can indeed be understood that the very high cost of the estate ("23 ducats for a single acre") had persuaded Giovanfrancesco Loredan to band together with "associates," who remain unidentified. However, in light of the document of December 14, 1545, it is possible to believe that in order to acquire the property, the nobleman used capital from the dowry of his wife Cornelia, a daughter of Giorgio Cornaro.[18] The Vespara property—the general topography of which can be visualized, thanks to a late Cinquecento map in the Correr Library in Venice (fig. I)—was promptly added to by Loredan who provided it with a house. The house, situated near the village of Fratta,[19] permitted him to follow closely the work of ordering and caring for the property. His tireless presence during the early part of 1531, at a time when a flooding of the Po menaced Canda and Vespara, is known.[20] And we have reason to believe that his great efforts and the extreme hardships he endured cost him his life.[21] Giovanfrancesco's estate remained in trust for his only son Giorgio,[22] then scarcely more than an adolescent (according to Barbaro,[23] he was born March 13, 1513), and for his three daughters. A little earlier one of the daughters, Maria, had married Gianfrancesco, son of Girolamo Giustiniani,[24] while the other two, Lucietta and Lucrezia, were unmarried. The latter had been affianced to Vincenzo (son of Antonio Grimani born on January 28, 1524[25]), who, having lost his father and being a minor,

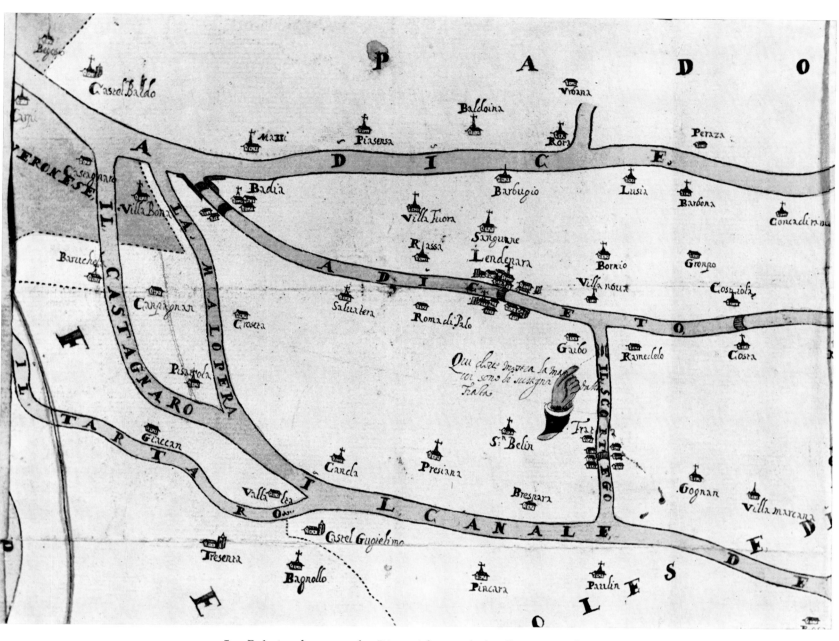

I - *Polesine between the River Adige and the Castagnaro Canal*
(from a late 16th century drawing). Venice, the Correr Library

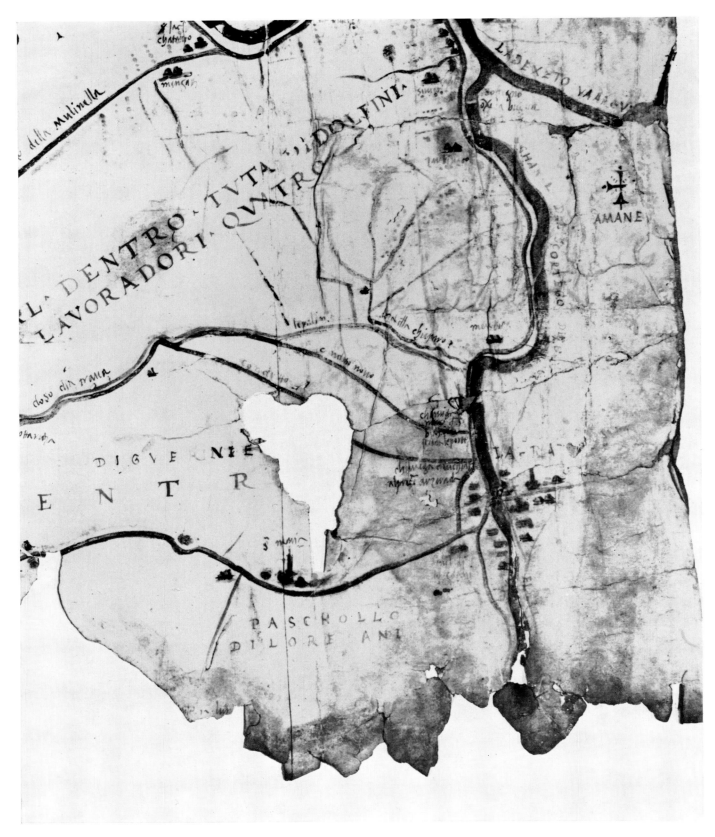

II - *Fratta and Valdentro* (from a drawing of 1549). Venice, State Archives

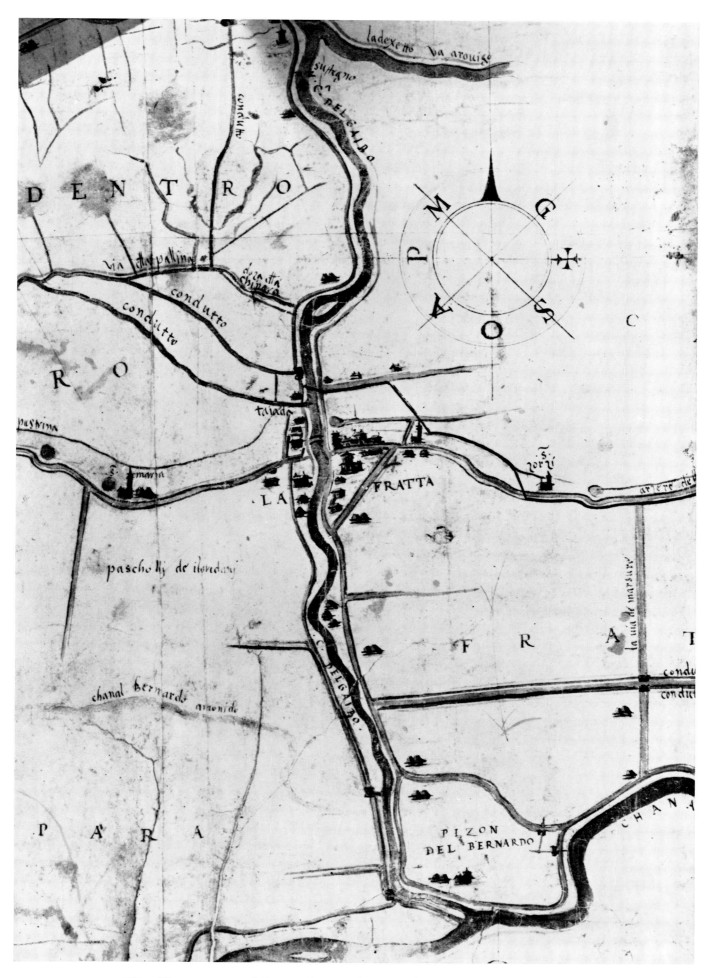

III - *The area around Fratta* (from a drawing of 1557). Venice, State Archives

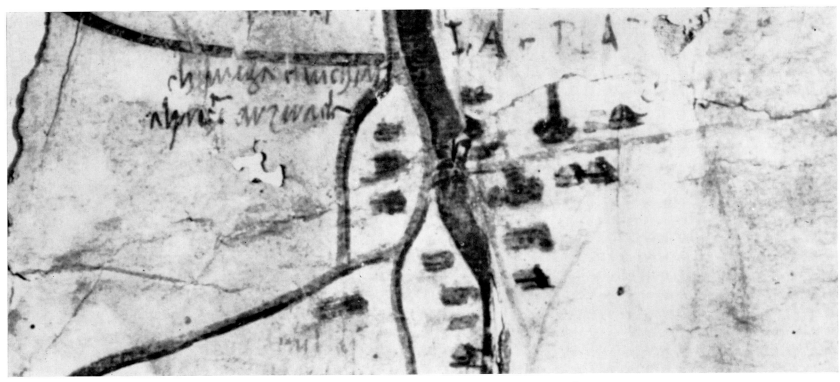

IV - *Fratta* (from a drawing of 1549). Venice, State Archives

V - *Fratta* (from a drawing of 1557). Venice, State Archives

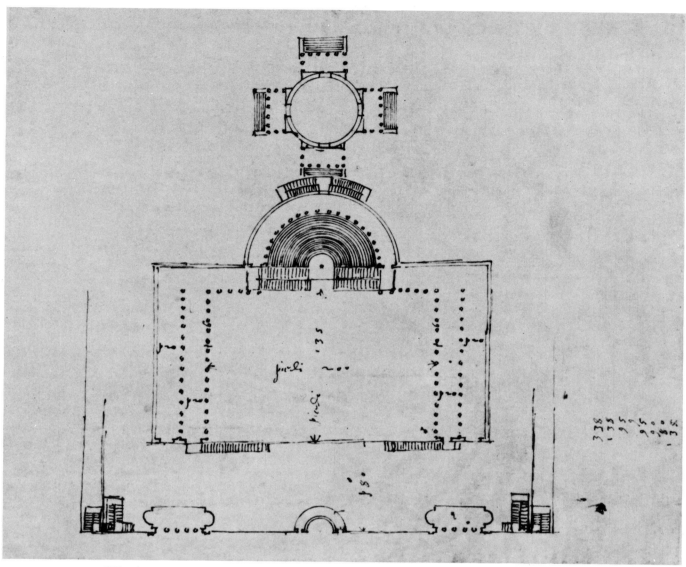

VI - Andrea Palladio, *Plan of the upper level of the Temple of Hercules at Tivoli.*
London, RIBA, IX, 8.

had been entrusted since 1529 by his grandfather (also named Vincenzo) and his mother Isabetta to none other than Giovanfrancesco Loredan. Loredan was asked to "treat him as your own son," and to act in the capacity of "tutor, guardian, and administrator."[26] There is proof that the young man collected his inheritance promptly and responsibly, and, as early as June 7, 1532, he was "in residence in Villa Fratta, jurisdiction of Rovigo" and engaged in buying a parcel of land "located in the lower part of Vespara in the Rovigo district." His intention was to increase the great holdings he had inherited.[27] In the succeeding years up to 1534, he was often to be found in his house in Polesine.[28]

At this same time Giorgio had other and quite different preoccupations. In the last part of February in 1533, Sanudo records the establishment, through the efforts of "fourteen of our young nobles of the first rank," of a "Compagnia di Calza." The young men "witnessed the agreement before the notary Hironimo de Canal and called themselves the Compagnia di Cortesi." The name of "sier Zorzi Loredan q. sier Zuan Francesco q. sier Marco Antoni" appears among the promotors. Alongside his name we find that of "sier Francesco Ba-

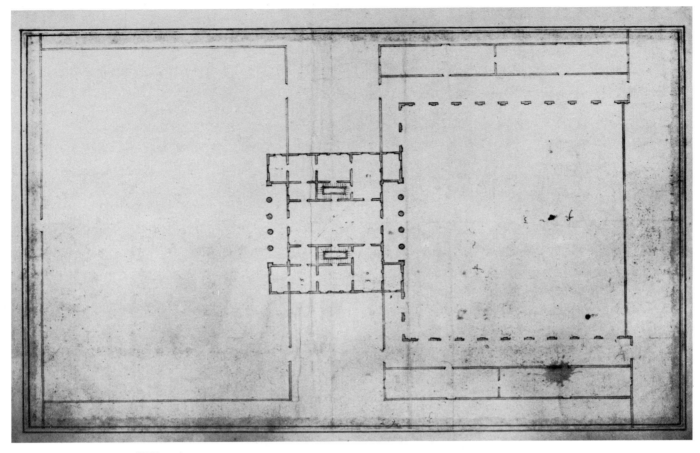

VII - ANDREA PALLADIO, *Study for Villa Mocenigo on the River Brenta.*
London, RIBA, XVI, 2.

doer di sier Pietro."[29] This then is the first testimony we have of an association. It will ultimately lead to the establishment of stronger ties.

On December 2, 1536 "magnificent lady Lucia Loredan, daughter of the most illustrious Miser Zuan Francesco," represented by the "magnificent messer Zorzi Loredan, her brother," was betrothed to the "magnificent messer Francesco Badoer, son of the most illustrious messer Piero."[30] The life of the Compagnia dei Cortesi in the meantime had extended itself with an increasing and sometimes turbulent succession of feasts, sumptuous spectacles, dinners, regattas, and elegant ceremonies. The group did not seem to be compromised by clear signs of popular discontent (or by "some of its enemies and emulators" as mentioned by Sanudo[31]) or the distrustfulness evidenced by the visitor from Ferrara.[32] On the con-

trary, the Cortesi, with an eye toward procuring prestigious ceremonial titles, did not hesitate to invite Francesco d'Este to become a member. He accepted and was present at the grandiose celebration prepared in his honor and centered about a brilliant theatrical production that took place on June 8, 1533.[33] In May of the following year the Cortesi welcomed Renata d'Este, who had come to Venice on an official visit.[34] It was a mark of political support and protection, alluded to in the documents and the sources.[35] Giorgio Loredan apparently was one of the most active of the leading spirits in these undertakings. He was soon to become the *Camerlengo* of the company with "sier Francesco Badoer" remaining at his side.[36] Loredan was sent by the Cortesi to the d'Este ambassador because the Company wished to invite the Duke of Ferrara to enter into their association.[37] And it was Lo-

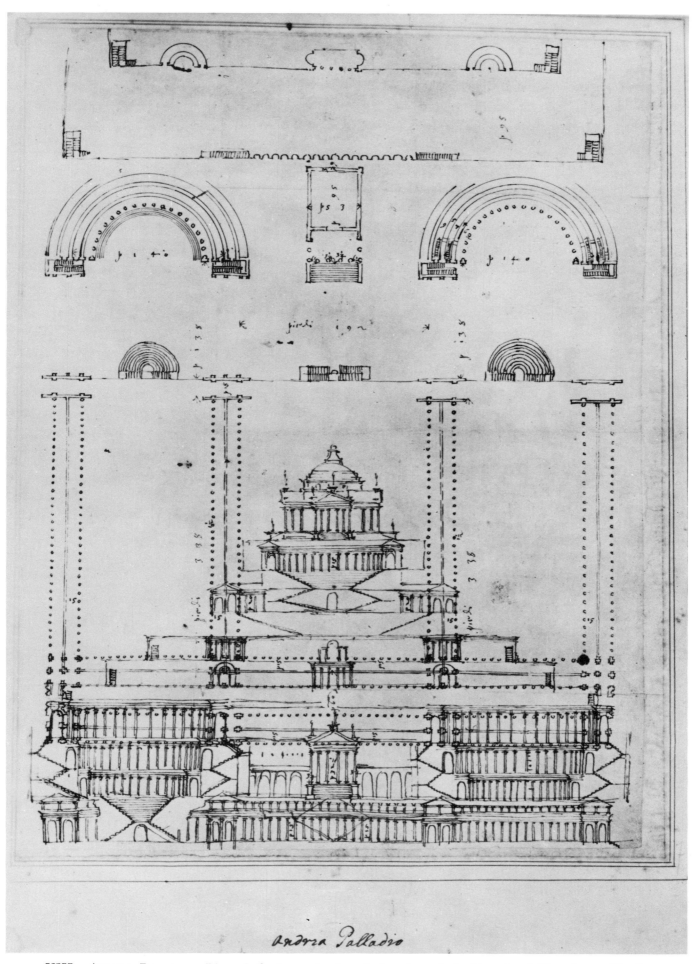

VIII - Andrea Palladio, *Plan of the lower level and elevation of the Temple of Hercules at Tivoli.*
London, RIBA, IX, 7.

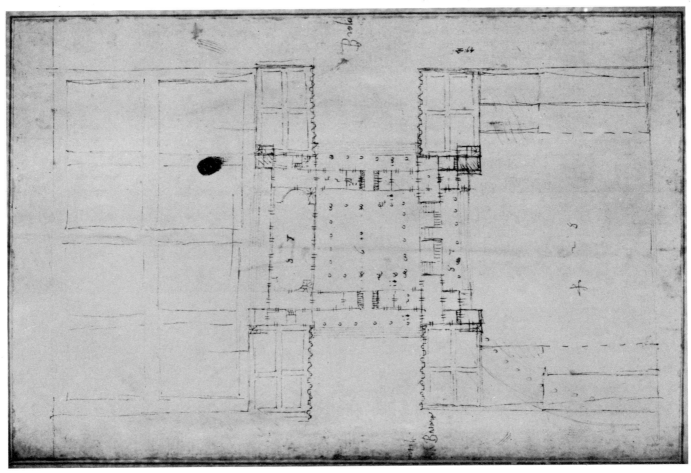

IX - ANDREA PALLADIO, *Studies for Villa Mocenigo on the River Brenta*. London, RIBA, X, 1 v.

redan who, according to all evidence, proffered the homage of the Compagnia to Francesco d'Este when he came to Venice on June 8, 1533.[38]

But these gay adventures could not go on forever. From a close reading of a contemporary report it can be learned that the marriage of Giorgio Loredan to Caterina Foscolo on February 4, 1536, signaled a final leave-taking of the gentlemen companions and at the same time a change of interests.[39] Moreover, Giorgio Loredan had only a short time to live; on October 6, 1538, at scarcely twenty-six years of age, he died.[40] The estate he left, which is registered in the declaration presented to the *Estimo* of 1537 on April 30, 1538, is an imposing one. Along with "mansions," "smaller houses," and "storehouses" in Venice—in the districts of S. Tomà, S. Paolo, S. Matteo,

S. Marcuolo, S. Casciano, S. Vito ("51 small houses")—as well as in Murano and Torcello, we note arable land in the Padua area, pastures near Cavarzere, and lastly, the great estate "in Polesine di Rovigo" situated "by the Crespara."[41] It is very doubtful that Loredan left a will,[42] and it is certain that he left no descendants. Thus the division of the estate was complicated and difficult. Lacking precise evidence, it would be reasonable to assume that the properties were at first transferred to his wife. The tax books relative to the *Estimo* of 1537 carefully record the assumption of "one-tenth" by "Donna Caterina Foscholo, widow of Ser Zorzi Loredan," charging to her name the share that had been her husband's.[43] However, a portion of the estate in Polesine had to bear the capital lien which supposedly had been deducted, on the occasion of the

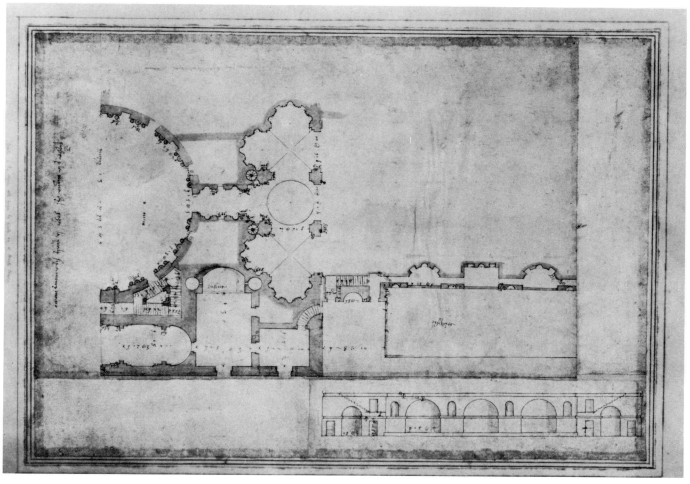

X - ANDREA PALLADIO, *Plan of Villa Madama.* London, RIBA, X, 18.

acquisition of the land, by using the dowry of his mother who was very likely still alive.[44] It was an unstable, precarious situation which depended on the survival, or the decision to remarry, of two women. The document of December 14, 1545, which begins the long digression, testifies by its date that in one way or another a decision had been made to ask for the division of the most complex of the land holdings—those of Vespara. On one side were Girolamo and Giovanni Cornaro, brothers of Giovanfrancesco Loredan's widow,[45] and on the other side, represented by their respective husbands, were Lucietta and Lucrezia Loredan who, in a separate meeting, had settled all questions with their sister Marietta.[46] Obviously, the concern here is not with tracing how they fared in the division of the inheritance, but to observe and fix the chronolo-

gical boundaries which these documents furnished and to look ahead to another important chronological signpost.

In March of 1548, Francesco Badoer became the owner of new houses in "San Vido," which he acquired through his brother-in-law.[47] The silence concerning acquisitions in Polesine that followed is due to the well-known tendency of the Venetian aristocracy to avoid taxes.[48] With the settlement of the Cornaro claims, it is clear that the Loredan sisters (and their husbands who constantly represented them, to the point of acting for them on their own account) made arrangements—within the context of the distribution of the entire estate—to divide the property in Polesine. Since the signing of the pacts characteristically occurred in different places ("in his own house" by Giovanni Cornaro at S. Angelo;[49]

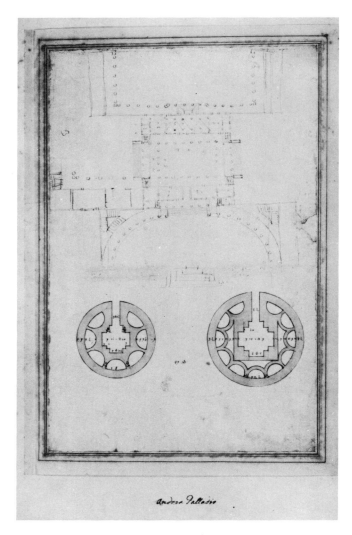

XI - ANDREA PALLADIO, *Study for Villa Mocenigo
on the River Brenta.* London, RIBA, X, 2 r.

by Vincenzo and Lucrezia Grimini "in their own house" at S. Agnese; by Francesco and Lucietta Badoer "in their own house" in S. Ermagora and Fortunato[50]), this intention had been implied at the time of the agreement with the Cornaro family. In any case, it seems that the action was completed during 1548, when on April 26 "in Villa Fratte in the house where the magnificent and generous Signor Vincenzo Grimani resides" the aforementioned noble acquired a smaller house in the area of Bragola. It is therefore possible to maintain that in the meantime he came into possession of the manor house built by the Loredan family near the populated area of Fratta and decided to provide it with more space and new

architectural features.[51] Thanks to two precise maps of the area (which are to be found in the State Archives of Venice, and which we will discuss in more detail [52]), one a map of 1549 (fig. II) and the other of 1557 (fig. III), the house can be placed in the lower part of the inhabited area of Fratta on the left of the Scortico. This explains the later expansion toward Bragola, which is easily identifiable in the zone between the village of S. Maria and Fratta in the map reproduced in fig. III.

On the same date, April 26, 1548, Vincenzo Grimani and Francesco Badoer officially testified, in Vincenzo's house, to their role as consorts of Lucietta and Lucrezia, sisters of Giorgio Loredan, concerning a question of common interest relative to the "Vespara."[53] This indicates that at the division of the estate a piece of land had been set aside to be administered jointly. Confirmation is given by the statement made by the same two gentlemen to the *Estimo* of 1566, in which they declared that "in aforesaid holdings in the Vespara" there is "a piece of land held in common ... consisting of 260 acres called the Valle di Santa Maria." At the same time they complained—to explain the reasons for the lack of interest in it—that it is "subject to breaches in the Po, breaches in the canals, and rain; at present it cannot be sown, nor is any sort of crop obtained, but cattle are being brought in an effort to reclaim it."[54] If in the aforementioned maps of 1549 and 1557 (figs. II-III) this section is easily identifiable in the plot marked by the words "paschollo di Loredani" or "pascolli de i Loredani," it is more difficult to establish with what standards and in what manner the other holdings in Vespara were divided. From the *Estimo* records of 1566 we know that Vincenzo had 520 acres and Francesco Badoer 460 acres, the total of which, when we add in the pascolo, more or less compares to the data given in the document of December

14, 1545, of 1,112 acres.[55] Moreover, it can be ascertained through the tax records of Rovigo that Badoer obtained the land in the community of Costa.[56] In regard to its precise location, we can only guess, although with good reason, that Badoer was given the section of the holdings below the "pascholli" beginning from the "chanal Bernardi amonido," which is plainly indicated on the map of 1557 (fig. III). From the description of six parcels of land "in the Polesine di Rovigo" which came into the possession of the Provveditori sopra Camere (the government) by confiscation and was auctioned off on July 26, 1563, it emerges that "the monito canal called the Bernardo Canal [is held] at the present time by the Magnificent misser Francesco Badoer."[57] The precise reasons for maintaining that he had also obtained a modest piece of land in the section above the "pascholli," along the boundaries of Bragola near Fratta beside the "built on" land, settled by his son-in-law, are obviously that he expected to build a proper country seat in a convenient location near an inhabited center and with easy access to communicating roads. Indeed, on May 6, 1580, Francesco Badoer's sons, "as heirs of the late Magnificent lady Lucieta their mother," freed themselves from a lease with which they had been encumbered since 1530, following a legal action by the "late most enlightened Zuan Francesco Loredano father of the aforesaid late lady Lucieta" against "their land on which, in the Villa della Fratte, they hold and possess very noble buildings and palaces."[58]

The agreement between Grimani and Badoer must have been peaceful since the two continued to maintain a friendly relationship, reinforced from time to time by mutually advantageous opportunities. The observation must be made (the reasons for it will be made clear) that Francesco was not as prompt as his relative in visualizing the potential economic advantage involved in

the acquisition, from which sprang that imponderable future opportunity. Thus, while Vincenzo quickly set out to expand his own land holdings with further important purchases,[59] following the same path as the Cornaro family,[60] Badoer was much slower and more cautious. The decision to undertake the construction of a residence of an unusual type is connected to the moment when all restrictions were dissolved and to the moment of the final choice, which was linked to the desire to render homage, in works and experiences, to the memory of the association of young adventurers, who were later to become relatives of one another.

Looking ahead to considerations which will develop later, it is necessary to emphasize the great significance of the presence, in the decorative scheme of the residence then being erected, of the coats of arms of Loredan (fig. XX) and Badoer (fig. XIX) and of the two crests joined together of the Badoer-Loredan alliance (fig. XXI). Nevertheless, the exact date when the villa was erected remains unknown. The documents provide only partial and uncertain answers, though they do at least permit us to circumscribe to a considerable degree the actual chronology. Continuing our search for valid answers on the archival level (the level that concerns us at present), we note that Burger proposes a date around the year 1566 on the completely inadequate basis of the *Estimo* declaration of that year.[61] By utilizing a wider spectrum of information, the date can be fixed at about 1560.[62] More recently Zorzi, by a subjective forcing of objective data, pushes the date even further back, as far as 1548, a date earlier proposed by Muraro without explicit reasons.[63] It is regrettable that only a gap in the records of the Provveditori sopra Camere prevents what would probably be a decisive resolution of this problem. The possibility that the previously cited purchase in 1566 of a parcel of land "in ... Bragola"[64] can be referred to the building project and can be directly related to the need to increase the modest piece of land that came from the Loredan inheritance is very convincing. This land was, generally speaking, suitable for a manor house because of its location, but more land added to it would have provided enough space to guarantee the possibility of laying out gardens, orchards, and land for cultivation so that the remote habitation, relatively distant from the bulk of the property, could be self-sufficient. From 1571 to 1681 that modest piece of land is recorded on the maps both by itself and as the seat of the villa.[65] Unfortunately, however, the deed of purchase cannot be traced.[66] It is therefore necessary to explore other sources.

We note, first of all, that the villa already existed in 1566 when on June 7 it was stated that "in Fratta, in the house of the magnificent Signor Francesco Badoer," in the presence of "Giacomo Castaldi of Piedmont" and a magistrate of the *Beni Inculti* (uncultivated lands), two pacts regarding questions about repairing the embankments were discussed.[67] And, very probably, the Villa existed in 1564 when Campo's *Diario*, which has come down to us through G. Silvestri's summaries, refers on July 3 and July 15 to the breaches "in the banks of the Scortico (the branch of the Adige which flows through the countryside in front of the villa) of Fratta." The reinforcement of the banks was taken care of a couple of years later, and not by chance, at a high level meeting in the residence of the gentleman threatened by the inadequate provisions against flooding.[68] On the other hand, it can be stated with certainty that Badoer had not established his permanent residence in 1548. On the occasion mentioned earlier regarding his presence in the Polesine in 1548, he was the guest of his son-in-law.[69] The large map dated 1549 in the State Archives of Venice, which we have so often utilized,[70] shows buildings of mod-

est importance within the narrow strip of land connected by a bridge to the inhabited area of Fratta and open to the low lying areas where the villa was to be erected. A vain attempt was made to identify the remains of the Castle of Salinguerra, mentioned by Palladio,[71] among these buildings. The inclination is to dismiss the possibility that Francesco had overcome the delays to prepare the land for building by 1553, since he was absent from the debate that led in that year to the beginning of the dredging of the river bed of the Scortico (or Gaibo) which was silted up and subject to overflowing—a detriment to the surrounding countryside.[72] Nevertheless, four years later the decisive events must have occurred. In answer to a decree of the Venetian Senate promulgated on December 27, 1556, the proprietors of the land situated in the low lying areas around Lendinara were called together on January 4 of the following year in order "to work, to act, to come to a common agreement, concerning the reclamation of the Valli di Valdentro, San Biagio and other nearby places,"[73] and together to see to the drainage of the wide marshy areas identifiable in the map of 1549 (fig. II). The petition to the Provveditori ai Beni Inculti for state aid[74] was quickly transmitted and received a quick reply. On February 15, 1556 (1557—Venetian reckoning), the Magistrates assigned the engineers Nicolò dal Cortivo and Giacomo Castaldo to make a survey of the lowlands to be reclaimed. On March 8 they presented a detailed drawing of the lowlands and on March 30 a complete report.[75] For our purposes it is not necessary to give a detailed explanation of what took place. The problem was resolved by a gigantic operation, involving the construction of a bridge canal under the upper reaches of the Scortico and of a long drainage canal toward S. Giorgio and Frattesina, and by the establishment of a consortium of the proprietors with an interest in the undertaking. One thousand two hundred acres were made available to them while the State assumed ownership of another 1,200 acres, these last to be sold at auction when the reclamation was well advanced and the value of the land had increased as a consequence.[76] The absence of Badoer's name from the list of the members of the consortium which was presented to the Provveditori on August 23, 1564,[77] need not indicate his indifference to an efficacious development of the low lying land of Polesine, but only, and provisionally, his indifference to the reclamation of the Valdentro. He turned his attention to this some time later, when in 1570 he bought at auction a section of the acreage remaining in the hands of the State.[78] We can understand that his first concern was for the systemization of Vespara. Moreover, the dredging of the Scortico in 1553, which made the water course available as an avenue of communications, and the successive action decided in 1557 increased the feasibility of utilizing the area for the construction of a villa. Thus we note that on December 6, 1563, Marcantonio Cornaro, son of the now deceased Giovanni Cornaro, Vincenzo Grimani, and Marcantonio Badoer, who was acting as a delegate for his father Francesco, met to complete, with the help of the Administration for the Uncultivated Lands, the reclamation of Vespara.[79] At that date, therefore, the presence of Badoer in the Polesine had to be a well established fact, based on a definitive residence. But there is more.

In the drawing we have referred to so often, which Nicolò da Cortino and Giacomo Castaldo showed the Venetian Provvedditori on March 8, 1557,[80] there are clear indications, in the area as yet undifferentiated in the map of 1549 (fig. IV), of the modifications that took place (fig. V). Zorzi reads these modifications as the level surface on which the villa was to be erected, but they could with justification be read as the

enclosing wall,[81] or a line of outbuildings. This would demonstrate, among other things, the compression of the building within the available space and would also explain the need to find some breathing room, which was provided at an undeterminable date by the acquisition of land at the bottom of Bragola. The indications on the map refer to construction work in progress, and certainly relate to the villa, if the unequivocal axial position of the small bridge over the Scortico is considered and if account is taken of the meticulousness of the cartographers. Giacomo Castaldo, one of the cartographers, was, in 1566, engaged in a personal relationship with Badoer.[82]

The date that has finally been reached for Villa Badoer—that of 1557—presupposes a reference to the project in 1556 which will be discussed in the next chapter. It also finds corroborative support, if any should be needed, in the fact that Francesco, having passed the turning point of the 1550s, undertook a consolidation or renovation of his own land holdings beginning in Venice. On June 16, 1551, for example, he made a declaration to the *Estimo* "that he had built in the district of San Vido."[83] There are only a few postscripts to be added. Francesco Badoer belonged (as has been observed throughout this study) to those social groups which were forming into a ruling political class. The formation of these groups took place following the reverses of the League of Cambrai and of the Levant, which later, after the opening of the Atlantic route and the revolution of prices, turned their initiative toward the maintenance of the *status quo* in international relations. The change in function of the League of Cambrai and the Levant corresponded to a hardening of the new ruling political class as an aristocracy and to a consolidation through land capitalization of the economic base of their power.[84] In other words, Badoer belonged to the period in Venice of the "failure of the bourgeoisie,"[85] which on a conscious level sees the affirmation of "sacred agriculture" and the concrete action of Alvise Cornaro, the promotor of state intervention in the *rentière* involution of the economy.[86] The ideological attitude and political commitment of Cornaro display the vital seeds of the precedent progressive bourgeois culture, seeds which were evident in the realistic and pragmatic attitude towards the "sober life." This in turn is influenced by the rhetoric of "country life" which came about when form was given to space in the heraldic organism of Pio Enea degli Obizzi's Cataio Palace, or in the Arcadian, and even hermetic, dimensions of Triffon Gabriele, Ramusio, and Bembo. But that is complementary, not contradictory, to the urban rhetoric of *renovatio imperii* and to the myth about Venice, universally proclaimed by the new political class, which has been studied by Tafuri with subtle insight.[87] At the same time, the presence, on a superstructural level, of a current that persisted dialectically in a phase that constituted a transition to an arrangement that was decisively aristocratic was expressed by Gramsci as "a truly popular national ... expression of the [15th century Venetian] bourgeoisie" and of the "regal, courtly, a-national" values characterizing the classes that had been put to the test by the recent historical vicissitudes. But this current of old bourgeois values was undermined and destined to be gradually reduced in the exclusive affirmation of the aristocratic class to the freezing of the structural process of "refeudalization." The indications are substantial. One thinks of the polemics about language which throws into relief with brilliant terminological clarity the movement to substitute an a-national instrument of cosmopolitan significance (a "neutral" Italian, but at the same time a class barrier—in function a substitute for Latin) for a popular national patrimony represented by the

dialect (once relevant to an "entity" but by now fragmented, discredited, and slowly reduced to the means of expression of the subordinate classes). At that time there was also evidence of this separation in the world of the theatre. On one side were the poets involved in the theatre, men such as Calmo, Venier, and Ruzante with their sometimes ambiguous patronage and alliances. On the other side were the literati, poets such as Bembo and Aretino, who were decisively supported and favored by the aristocracy.[88] The role of the Compagnia della Calza was symptomatic. On this subject (which found in the theatre its most congenial field of expression) it represented, more generally, the aspirations (not only cultural) of the new political elite.

It would be worthwhile to go more deeply into the analysis from the point of view of such an interpretation. And on this subject, the study of Lionello Venturi remains fundamental.[89] First of all, he carefully examined the origins and the connections of the promotors and leading spirits. They were, at first glance, the young and the very young belonging to the families most active in the transactions that we have summarily described. In the modes of expression, over and above a mere tenuous appearance of hedonism, they are wellrooted and solid, by now ingrained, one might say, with a cosmopolitan outlook, with a taste for sumptuous self-celebration, and with a tendency to conceive of the values of culture as "clad with nobility and riches and other extrinsic ornaments"—to quote Paruta.[90] We note finally a great change in the consciousness and habits that, in respect to the complex situation and objective compromises of their forebears, took place on this reclaimed land ("the finest and most fitting business for gentlemen is to buy land," according to Roberto di Spilimburgo), a firmer attitude without ambiguity.

The episodes to which I have briefly

b. - Giallo Fiorentino, *A grotesque on the north wall of the central hall*

referred regarding the adventures of the Cortesi thus take on an emblematic and illuminating prominence. They trace at some distance, but along lines which can be deciphered, the personality of Francesco Badoer, who, insofar as it was he who gave the commission for the villa, has a significance that cannot be treated lightly. Also, we have a valid explanation of the delays noted in his decision to begin the major undertaking involved in building a manor house in Polesine, "the promised land"— according to Agostinetti, appropriately quoted by Ventura.[91] It was called "the promised land" because of the fertility of its soil and the availability of farm workers at low wages, providing a tremendous op-

portunity for a profitable operation. But it was also an unhealthy land, difficult because of the scarcity of main roads and because of the extremes in weather from cold to heat. Therefore it was not well adapted to an architectural undertaking that expressed the myth of "the life on the land" in an edifying and splendid manner. To bring together both the economic and the rhetorical aspects, charged in this instance with endless intimate implications and memories, it was not by chance that Badoer called in Palladio who in those years was experimenting with and developing his own "classicism"— a classicism adapted to the ambience of his patronage: the Venetian aristocracy.[92]

NOTES TO CHAPTER I

[1] G. VASARI, 1568, vol. VII, p. 530; A. PALLADIO, 1570, L. II, p. 48.

[2] F. BURGER, 1909, p. 111; G. G. ZORZI, 1969, p. 94.

[3] See especially M. BARBARO, *Famiglie nobili*, ms., 43 r (from which it appears that Francesco was the second son of Piero, and remember that the ÖNB codex of the various versions of Barbaro is the most authoritative); M. BARBARO, *Discendenze patrizie*, ms., at the relative entry; M. BARBARO, *Arbori de Patritii*, ms., c. 68 r; G. A. CAPPELLARI VIVARO, *Il Campidoglio Veneto*, ms., vol. I, at the relative entry. We also learn that he had a sister who married Alvise Emo and that his brother Angelo was the prior of S. Giovanni Evangelista in Venice. No information is furnished by the *Nascimento*, ms., passim.

[4] G. A. CAPPELLARI VIVARO, *Il Campidoglio*, ms., vol. I, at the relative entry.

[5] Cf., above all, M. BARBARO, *Nozze*, ms., c. 248 bis (1536: "la figlia de ser Zuanfrancesco [Loredan] quondam ser Marcantonio quondam ser Zorzi in ser Francesco Badoer de Piero quondam ser Albertino").

[6] G. A. CAPPELLARI VIVARO, *Il Campidoglio*, ms., vol. I, at the relative entry. See also, among others, the genealogy enclosed in the volume marked I in ASV. *Privati: Badoer* (in a loose sheet).

[7] The date is in *Necrologio de' nobili* (ms., on c. 12 v, December 1572) and is confirmed by a document precisely datable 1572, to which we will return, wherein the death, probably at the end of the year, is noted (ASV. *X Savi alle Decime: Catastici del Dogado e della Terraferma* reg. 450, c. 367 r), while in a document of December 16, 1571, to which we will also return, he seemed to be still alive (ASV. *Provveditori sopra Camere*

reg. B I 10, c. 48 v), as in the other *carta* of February 27, 1571 (1572 - Venetian reckoning): ASV. *X Savi allè Decime: Redecima* 1566. Condizioni aggiunte b. 151.

[8] See D. BELTRAMI, 1961, pp. 45-100; G. LUZZATTO, 1961, pp. 152-262; S. J. WOOLF, 1962; A. DE MADDALENA, 1964; B. PULLAN, 1968; A. VENTURA, 1968.

[9] *Necrologio de' Nobili*, ms., c. 11 v.

[10] ASV. *X Savi alle Decime: Redecima* 1537 b. 132, Stipulation n. 297 and *ibid., idem, Redecima* 1537 reg. 1476, c. 974 (the division was actually reported only on March 28, 1554: the document, witnessed by the notary Nicolò Stella, cannot be traced. It can be stated that before Piero's death his sons' economic circumstances enabled them to act autonomously; insofar as Francesco is concerned we will cite various facts; in regard to Andrea, for example, see BCV. Mss. *Dandolo*, PD c. 936/160, etc.

[11] G. PRIULI, ed. 1941, p. 50. The commitment of the Venetian aristocracy to landed property was in actuality gradual and began as far back as the 15th century (cf., for example, V. LAZZARINI, 1949 and 1960, G. CHERUBINI, 1967, and A. VENTURA, 1968); in reference to the interests of the historians of the "villa" see the implicit, polite controversy between M. ROSCI, 1968, and A. VENTURA, 1969, and for a concrete exemplification—earlier considered by RUPPRECHT, 1963—L. PUPPI, 1969.

[12] ASV. *X Savi alle Decime: Redecima* 1566 b. 132, Stipulation n. 217 (and cf. *ibid., idem,* reg. 370, c. 1969 r, n. 297).

[13] *Ibid.*

[14] BCV. Mss. PD c. 2661/3, cc. 75 r - 88 r: it is a copy (another copy is in BCV. Mss. PD 2346/VII in a *Miscellanea di carte e disegni relativi al retratto della Vespara*) of the original notarial attestation which is not among the documents (a few

sheets of parchment) that have come to us from the notary Bonifacio Soliano (now in ASV). The document attests that the survey was done "secondo il disegno di tutto il luogo fatto per Domenego dall'Abaco pertegador della Magnifica Comunità di Padoa." Here is the most interesting passage: "magnifici et clarissimi viri domini Hieronimus et Joannes Cornelio fratres quondam magnifici et clarissimi domini Georgii equitis et procuratoris Sancti Marci Venetiarum ac uterque pro portione sua ex una, et nobiles viri domini Franciscus Baduario filius magnifici et clarissimi domini Petri et Vincentius Grimani quondam magnifici domini Antonii ... agentes sciliscet prefactus [sic] dominus Franciscus nomine ac vice domine Luiete uxoris sue ... et prefactus [sic] dominus Vincentius nomine ac vice nobilis domine Lucretie uxoris sue ... ambarum sororum et filiarum quondam magnifici domini Joannis Francisci Lauredano intervenientium uti succetricum et sive in hereditarium nomine quondam viri nobilis domini Georgii Lauredano fratris ipsarum pro portionibus suis ... ex altera," "ritrovandosi haver tra loro per indiviso ... del bosco et presa della Vespara zoé [ciascuna parte] per la mittà," declare to have "fatto veder, mesurar ... detti beni et luoghi per persone pratiche et periti et [che] quelli han diviso in due parte equalmente."

15 ASV. *Senato*: Terra reg. 20, cc. 183 r and v (the deliberation is completely reported by M. SANUDO, 1496-1533, vol. XXVI, cll. 497-499). The deliberation states that the sales will be carried out "cum quella forma che parerà esser de mazor avantazo de la Signoria nostra, vendendo parte a parte, e delivrando a chi più offerirà ...," remaining firm that "non se intendi ferma alcuna vendeda se non la sarà ballotada et approbada per el Collegio nostro cum intervento de li Capi del Consiglio nostro di, si come se observa ne le vendede de l'officio del fischo, et habia almeno do terzi de le ballote."

16 An abundant documentation is in ASV, *Provveditori sopra Camere*, passim. Cf., in any case, A. CAPPELLINI, 1925, passim, and the lucid indispensable resume by B. RIGOBELLO, 1964, pp. 14-17.

17 The document comes to us from the copy taken from the original document of the notary Giulio Zilioli of July 27, 1592: BCV. Ms. PD 2346/VII. It specifies "14 supradicti mensis. In Collegio cum dominis capitibus illustrissimi Consilii X, quod haec venditio approbetur et fuit approbata." The property is thus described: "tutte le valli, dossi, mote, boschivi et di qualunque altra qualità esser si voglia ... nel loco della Vespara, il qual ha diverse parti, overo lochi, che hanno diversi nomi, con tutti li suoi canali, fra tutti li suoi confini situati nella giurisdition et pertinentie del Polesene di Rovigo, li quali tutti lochi della Vespara predetta posson essere campi 2000 alla misura padovana, o più o meno."

18 M. BARBARO, *Arbori*, ms., c. 333 r; G. A. CAPPELLARI VIVARO, *Il Campidoglio*, ms., vol. II, c. 232 r. The dotal pact has not been found.

19 ANR. *Giacomo Celega q. Domenico*: Busta atti 1524-1531. Quaderno January 2 - December 31, 1531, c. 23 r (May 1, 1531: "in villa Frate iurisditionis Rhodigii in domo habitationis ... clarissimi domini Joannis Francisci Lauredani"). For a hypothetical reconstruction of the building see the observations of B. RUPPRECHT, 1964, and M. ROSCI, 1968.

20 M. SANUDO, 1496-1533, vol. LV, cll. 113, 120, 132; see also, vol. LI, cl. 627.

21 *Necrologio de' nobili*, ms., c. 127 r. CAPPELLARI VIVARO (*Il Campidoglio*, ms., vol. II, c. 228 v) errs where he registers the death of the gentleman in 1534. The information of BARBARO (*Arbori*, ms., c. 233 r) is correct when he states that Giovanfrancesco was buried in S. Chiara at Murano before the altar of St. Francis, while Cappellari Vivaro stated that the tomb was in S. Andrea della Certosa.

22 The will of Giovanfrancesco Loredan has not been traced, in spite of persistent research in the ASV (for example, Notarile: Indici. Serie II: *Testamenta virorum*, vol. XX [1528-1543: noncupativi], vol. XXX [1528-1569: cedole]; or among the Commissarie deposited at the Provveditori de Citra, Supra e Ultra; or among the details of will in the holdings of the Inquisitori alle Acque, etc.); and, therefore, it is likely that he died intestate.

23 M. BARBARO, *Arbori*, ms., c. 333 r.

24 M. SANUDO, 1496-1533, vol. LIV, cl. 304. February 20,

1531: "In questo zorno fo compito le noze di sier Zuan Francesco Justinian di sier Hieronimo procurator in la fia di sier Zuan Francesco Loredan quondam sier Marco Antonio, con dota ducati 10 milia, bellissima zovene. Vene fuora vestita di restagno d'oro, con una zoia di seda con zoie e perle che picava e con li capelli zo per le spalle bellissimi." In attendance were thirteen procurators and three brothers-in-law of the groom, "sier Zuan de Leze, sier Vetor Grimani, sier Vincenzo Grimani," the last named being the grandfather of the Vincenzo with whom we are concerned.

25 M. BARBARO, *Arbori*, ms., c. 146 r; M. BARBARO, *Discendenze*, ms., c. 90 v; the ÖNB version is on the other hand generic; M. BARBARO, *Famiglie*, ms., cc. 195 r and v.

26 ASV. *Avogaria de Comun* reg. 145/6, c. 137 r ff., on January 15, 1529. Giorgio Loredan's father died in 1527. Very probably the decision to place Giorgio under guardianship was due to that fact. For Isabetta's role in the history of Palazzo Grimani in S. Maria Formosa, cf. R. GALLO, 1960, pp. 157-158.

27 ANR. *Giacomo Celega q. Domenico*: Busta atti 1531-1555, Quaderno January 1-December 27, 1532, cc. 47 r and 64 r.

28 *Ibid., idem.*, Quaderno January 15-December 31, 1533, cc. 2 r, 49 r; Quaderno January 13 - December 14, 1534, cc. 9 v, 10 r and v, 11 r and v. Some of the documents concern acquisitions in "Brespara."

29 M. SANUDO, 1499-1533, vol. LVII, cl. 550: the day celebrating the foundation of the Company, in May 1533, is described in vol. LVII, cll. 183-84. The head of the Company is "Agostino Querini quondam Zuone de Stampalia." The inaugural festivities, held in May, were lavish; they began with a religious ceremony in S. Maria Formosa ("la qual era tanto piena che non si poteva star") "con soni, canti, musica excellentissima" of a precious organ and with "un'oration vulgar in laude di la compagnia" given by "pre' Francesco Rizo, loro capelan," before the swearing in of the twenty-one members. After the Mass ("che fo molto solenne, et za più anni non è sta fata una simile nel mondo"), the companions "andono per tera con le trombe et soni et servitori con bastoni in man avanti a S. Marco," and then, after lunch, they rendered homage to the Council. The festivities ended in the evening with "un festin a la Zueca in cha Vendramin, caxa de loro compagni [a Polo Vendramin] et se farà al fresco soto el portego." Naturally the companions had provided for a uniform and the times when it should be worn.

30 ASV. *Avogaria de Comun* reg. 143/4, cc. 21 v - 22 v. The dowry assigned to Lucietta was 10,000 ducats to be paid in installments.

31 For example, the boats that were to be used for the inaugural festivities were damaged; "parole [erano state] scrite sopra li muri in suo vituperio" or "parole vergognose contro di loro": M. SANUDO, 1496-1533, vol. LVIII, cll. 183, 189, and 232. The Cortesi reacted by applying to the Capi del Consiglio dei Dieci and posting a price of 200 ducats on the head of the persons responsible.

32 ASMo. *Segreto Estense*: Cancelleria Estero. Ambasciatori b. 31. The ladies many of whom were invited to the celebrations of the Cortesi, tended to fail to turn up. Caterino Zeno, a resident wrote on June 26, 1533, "e perché son gioveni e con qualche costume giovanile". The negotiations for the invitation to Francesco are referred to by Caterino Zeno in dispatches of May 6, 22, and 29, 1533. The festivities of June 8 are fully related by M. SANUDO (1496-1533, vol. LVIII, cll. 263-264) where he describes the spectacle acted out on an installation "fatto far sopra do piate grande," like "una macchina bellissima di legname in tondo, coperta et torniata di sopra di tele biave con alcune corde dorade che la teniva, et fato a quadri con banche in mezo in forma de teatro" (the chronicler adds that "imagination de tal machina et artificio è stato uno maistro Domenego"). For an attempt at reconstruction, cf. L. PADOAN URBAN, 1966. We know that the theatre, between, "soni et canti" (and there is a "femena francese la qual balla ... sopra uno animal"), "fo menato per Canal grando fino a la porta de la Doana, dove si retene" (a little later, "li banchi over teatro di Compagni Cortesi" berthed "a la Zueca a la riva di cha Vendramin," will be destroyed by a storm), and the members moved "sin apresso il rio di San Polo a cha Loredan nel soler da basso, dove sier Vincenzo Grimani procurator [the

grandfather of the Vincenzo with whom we are concerned] li prestò la caxa da far la cena et compir la festa, la qual era ben conzada" (M. SANUDO, 1496-1533, vol. LVIII, cll. 264 and 350-351). I believe that the house referred to was the one that Francesco Badoer inhabited at a certain period (ASV. *X Savi alle Decime: Redecima* 1566 b. 132, n. 297: Francesco "sta al presente [June 28, 1556] in Contrà di S. Polo in casa della magnifica madonna Isabetta Grimani olim del magnifico messer Antonio").

33 ASMo. *Segreto Estense*: Cancelleria Estero. Ambasciatori b. 31.

34 ASMa. *Carteggio Estero*: Inviati a diversi b. 1468, in the dispatches of Benedetto Agnello of May 13, 16, and 23, 1534 (among other things "alcuni gioveni de la Compagnia de la Calza chiamata la Compagnia de Cortesi ... balarono anche essi sul bucintoro con le gentildonne de la signora duchessa"; and, alongside the Doge and the highest dignitaries, in their function as escorts of Renata, they appear almost continually.

35 See the accounts of the three precedent notes and ASMo. *Segreto Estense*: Cancelleria Estero. Ambasciatori b. 31 (dispatch of Zeno of May 9, 1533); M. SANUDO, 1476-1533, vol. LVII, cl. 550; vol. LVIII, cll. 358-359; etc.

36 M. SANUDO, 1496-1533, vol. LVIII, cl. 184.

37 ASMo. *Segreto Estense*: Cancelleria Estero. Ambasciatori b. 31. (Dispatch by Zeno of May 6, 1533: "Il mi fa grande instanza il magnifico Zorzi Loredan fo del magnifico messer Zuan Francesco ... ." The petition was made in the name "de tuti i sui compagni" to the resident in order that "volgari pregar [il signore] ad esser content[o] farli gratia acetarli per servitori et compagni."

38 *Ibid., idem.*, Ambasciatori b. 32: dispatch of G. B. Angiari of June 8, 1533; in the brief text we are given the colors of the Calza. This information will be helpful when we come to the problem of the decoration of the villa (see Pt. II, ch. I, n. 18). The "calcia" was offered "in un bacile d'argento."

39 ASMo. *Segreto Estense*: Cancelleria Estero, Ambasciatori b. 31. Zeno writes in a dispatch of February 4, 1536: "Questa sera se fa una gran festa de compagni dove se va redur un gran numero de donne et eri se maritò Zorzi Loredan in una Foscola [con oltre 20,000 ducati] de dotta, ma una puta assai più che bruta; per questo non dirò altro." For the dotal pact, see ASV. Avogaria de Comun reg. 143/4, cc. 273 v - 275 v. CAPPELLARI VIVARO (*Il Campidoglio*, ms., vol. II, c. 232 r) errs in alluding to a "Maria" di Nicolò (rather than Andrea) Foscolo.

40 M. BARBARO, *Discendenze*, ms., c. 212 v; *Necrologio de' nobili*, c. 127 v; etc.

41 ASV. *X Savi alle Decime: Redecima* 1537 b. 103, Condizione n. 704, and reg. 365, n. 704.

42 The investigation, like those made to track down the will of Giovanfrancesco Loredan, has been completely fruitless. Besides the silence of the most likely sources (ASV. *Notarile*: Indice. Serie II: *Testamenta virorum*, vol. XX [1528-1543: noncupativi] and vol. XXX [1528-1569: cedole] and Commissarie presso i Provveditori de Citra, Supra e Ultra; Inquisitori alle Acque), nothing appears among the documents, *ibid.*, of the Giudici del Proprio (reg. 5, 6, 7, 8, and 9) from 1530 to 1562.

43 ASV. *X Savi alle Decime* reg. 1475 ("Fia" of the Estimo of 1537), c. 735.

44 ASV. *X Savi alle Decime: Redecima* 1537 b. 103, Condizione n. 704 (on Aprile 30, 1538, Giorgio declares "in la Contrà di San Thomaso una casa da statio nela qual nel soler da basso abita [sua] madre").

45 In the document of distribution of 1545 (BCV. Mss. PD 2346/VII) we know that of the one-half share going to the Cornaro family one-third went to Girolamo as the "donee" and two-thirds to Giovanni as "residuario coherede universal del reverendissimo et bone memorie quondam monsignor messer Francesco suo fratello cardinal Corner del titolo di S. Proxida al qual per la division tra loro signori fratelli da cha Corner era toccado ditta mittà." For the Cornaro relationships cf. M. BARBARO, *Famiglie*, ms., c. 70 v (Francesco had obtained the cardinalate in 1528 from Clement VII for 38,000 ducats).

46 BCV. Mss. PD 2346/VII (refers to "division [già] fatta con sua sorella Marietta Giustignan").

47 ASV. *X Savi alle Decime: Redecima* 1537 b. 114, Condizione aggiunta n. 300. "Francesco Badoer de messer Piero [dà] per nota ... qualmente [abbia] accresuto de fito in certe caxe in contrà di San Vido a [lui] tochade per devision de beni che fu del quondam ser Zorzi Loredan fo [suo] cognado": ciò "... in execucion de la parte presa adì 29 marzo 1548" dall'autorità competente. Vincenzo Grimani alla sua volta denuncerà una serie di "adiunti" significativamente "in la contrà di San Vio" and "nella contrà de San Zeminian" ASV. *X Savi alle Decime: Redecima* 1537 b. 120, Condizione aggiunta ordinaria n. 1744).

48 The comparison between the "adjuncti" cited in the preceding note and the panorama described in the "condizioni" furnished to the Estimo of 1566 by Francesco and Vincenzo (respectively ASV. *X Savi alle Decime: Redecima* 1566 b. 132, Condizione n. 297 and b. 125, Condizione n. 624) is symptomatic.

49 BCV. Mss. c. 661/3, cc. 75 r - 88 r (for further information on the Cornaro distribution, see R. GALLO, 1960, pp. 114-116). It should be noted, in passing, that the S. Angelo palace is the edifice bought by Giovanni Cornaro from the Lando family on January 21, 1542 (ASV. *Quattro Ministeriali: Strida e clamori* reg. 122, c. 16 v., etc.), which in that same year was rearranged by Sanmicheli and Vasari (cf. L. PUPPI, 1971, p. 86) and was by 1545 in order. The witness to the signature of the Cornaros was a "ser Jacobo agnominato Florentino quondam ser Dominici de Este habitatore in loca della Fratta"; but this man, whose name might at first seem promising in an investigation of the villa of Fratta, is in actuality of small importance. I found that "Jacomo Florentin" was the "factor" of "miser Zuan Cornero" and secretary of the Compagnia del Sacramento di Fratta in the years 1551, 1552, and 1553 (APF. Busta segnata: *Libri 3 S. Sacramento: Libro de la fraternitta* .... [1550-1570], cc. 2 r and and 21 r; *Libro cassa* ... [1550-1582], c. III; etc.

50 BCV. Mss. PD 2661/3, cc. 75 r - 88 r.

51 ANR. *Franco Franchi q. Giovanni*: Busta anni 1536-1549, Quaderno January 13 - December 9, 1548, cc. 22 r - v (n. 449). It deals with "unam domunculam cum una tigeta de palia cum curte et horto positam in fundo Bragole jurisditionis Castriguglielmi ... pro se suisque filiis et heredibus." The allusion, in the specification of the boundaries of the property acquired, land belonging to Vincenzo Grimani ("magnifici domini emptoris"), confirms that the distribution had taken place. The location of that property near S. Bellino affirms that the tract to the east of Vespara must have gone to Grimani (see fig. I). Present at the notarial ceremony was "domino Jacobo Florentino filio quondam domini Dominici habitatore Frate" (see n. 49).

52 See nn. 70 and 80.

53 ANR. *Franco Franchi q. Giovanni*: Busta anni 1536-1549. Quaderno January 13 - December 9, 1548, cc. 23 r - 24 v (n. 450). The formula is always the same: "uti mariti et nomine nobilium et magnificarum dominarum Lucie et Lucretie, sorores atque uxores infrascriptorum Francisci et Vincentii et sorores et heredes quondam clarissimi domini Georgii Lauredano." The document is reported in ASV. *Privati: Badoer.*, vol. segnato II, c. 80 r; as regards the original attestation it seems to allude to a house in Fratta owned jointly by Grimani and Badoer.

54 ASV. *X Savi alle Decime: Redecima* 1566 b. 132, Condizione n. 624 (for Grimani). The "owned in common" character of the property is confirmed by a fragmentary drawing by Domenico Gallo dated "aprile 1565," where land near the church of S. Maria is plotted out (ASV. *Miscellanea Mappe* n. 181; the folio measures 448 mm. by 347 mm. and was executed on the order of the Provveditori sopra Camere). It records, in the lowlands of Vespara "un loco ditto el passcollo [sic!] possesso al presente ... per ... [i] magnifici Badoeri e Grimani."

55 See n. 54. Note, in particular, the designation of "passcollo."

56 The property is cited in Badoer's declaration of 1566 (see n. 12); however, it is registered as the property of the "magnifico messer Francesco Badoero," also by the fiscal authorities of Rovigo (ACR. Volume segnato *Perticazione 1570* reg. 57, cc. 59 v [126 r], 60 r [127 v], 60 v [127 r], on "30 zenaro 1567"). It should be noted that the same property was recorded in 1546 as the property of "li heredi del quondam magnifico messer Zan-

francesco Loredan" (ACR. Volume segnato *Perticazione 1546* [the note is deleted], cc. 50 v [142 r], 51 r [143 v], 51 v [143 r]: evidence that, in that year, the distribution had not yet taken place.

[57] ASV. *Provveditori sopra Camere* reg. B I 10, cc. 10 r e v, 13 r e v, 15 r.

[58] ANR. *Giacomo Antonio Colla*: Busta unica, Quaderno protocolli March 22, 1580 - March 17, 1581, cc. 9 r - 10 v (n. 188.) A copy of the document is in ASV. *Privati: Badoer*. Volume segnato II, cc. 21 v - 22 v. The pact of 1530, which would have been "per instrumento publico rogado il quondam messer Giacomo Celega nodaro già publico de Rovigo," has not been found.

[59] For the increases in the land holdings of the Grimani, see, besides the earlier cited Condizione 1566, the *partite* recorded in ASV. *X Savi alle Decime* reg. 1475, c. 771 v (concerning property left by Isabetta Grimani, September 19, 1554, and by Vetto Grimani, January 3, 1560) and reg. 1482, c. 1033 v (in these latter *partite* appear properties from the Emo family; in fact, Vincenzo, left a widower after the death of Lucrezia Loredan in 1557, married Andriana q. Giovanni Emo: M. BARBARO, *Discendenze*, ms., c. 90 v). Cf., finally, ASV. *Notarile: Testamenti*. Cesare Zilioli b. 1261, n. 891, where the codicil to the will of Vincenzo is found. It was dictated on June 20, 1567 (opened after his death on November 26, 1582). Vincenzo chose as executors his wife, his mother, "il reverendo messer Antonio Grimani," and "lo illustrissimo et reverendissimo messer Zan Grimani patriarcha d'Aquilegia," his uncle, who, at that date rented "sul Polesene de Rovigo in Pontichio ... una casa con uno brollo" (ASV. *X Savi alle Decime: Redecima 1566* reg. 368, cc. 901 r - 902 r, n. 574).

[60] From March 10, 1550, a "fabrica de Vespara" (APF. File marked *Libri 3 S. Sacramento: Libro cassa ...* [1550-1570], c. III) was functioning on behalf of Giovanni Cornaro, for which stone was procured, utilized in part in the renovation of the church in Fratta. For this edifice, like the Loredan-Grimani building (see n. 53) and in general the buildings belonging to the first phase of the Venetian expansion into land holdings in Polesine, it is difficult to imagine what the architectural elements looked like. An extension of the investigations of Rupprecht, Rosci, etc., in this area would have to be based on possible remains and on cartographic evidence.

[61] F. BURGER, 1909, p. 111. It is useful to emphasize that when we look for the presence of buildings in the country, the fiscal records are unfortunately silent, as are the wills. We do not have the will of Francesco Badoer and nothing is to be obtained from those of his sons: Marcantonio (ASV. *Privati: Badoer*. Volume marked II, cc. 87 v - 88 v, of June 1, 1588, but submitted to the Cancelleria Inferiore on May 19, 1593); Piero (*ibid., idem*, volume marked II, cc. 91 r - 92 v, of January 14, 1596); Giovanni (*ibid., Notarile: Testamenti*. Fabrizio Benazzano b. 57, n. 318, of September 30, 1609); Andrea (*ibid., idem*, Giulio Zilioli b. 1241, n. 64, of April 15, 1613: also two codicils, *ibid., idem*, Fabrizio Benazzano b. 56, n. 24, of July 11, 1618, and September 28, 1619).

[62] L. PUPPI, 1965-1966, pp. 50-57. The reasoning and the conclusions of the present writer have been received favorably by ACKERMAN, 1967, pp. 47-49. Moreover, in continuing the investigations, several corrections and refinements have been made without, however, markedly shifting the chronology.

[63] G. G. ZORZI, 1969, p. 96 (in his interpretation of the documents and also in relationship with other considerations, Zorzi joins the decision of erecting the villa to the births of Francesco's children, between 1544 and 1560); M. MURARO, 1954, p. 107.

[64] See n. 12.

[65] ASV. *X Savi alle Decime: Catastici del Dogado e della Terraferma* reg. 450 ("nella villa di Bragola campi 8, in nove, arativi, li quali fanno lavorar in casa et per la parte dominical" [ca 1572]; *ibid., Privati: Badoer*. Volume segnato I, Fascicolo entitled *1681 28 settembre: divisioni seguite per le 5 sorelle Badoer* ("il palazzo posto nella terra della Fratta ... il tutto in quantità di campi nove, quadrati uno, tavole sessanta nove"); *ibid., idem.*, Autograph attestation by the notary Antonio Petraz-

zolo q. Nicola di Rovigo of March 31, 1585 ("Frate in contracta ubi dicitur Bragolla territorio Rhodigii im [sic!] pallatio clarissimorum dominorum de cha Badoero nobilium venetorum"), etc.

[66] ASV. *Provveditori sopra Camere*, passim. Although carefully explored, no information was found in the records of the Governatori alle Pubbliche Entrate or of the X Savi alle Decime.

[67] ASV. *Provveditori sopra Beni Inculti: Processi, Investiture* b. 46, in file entitled *Lendinara Retratto* (Reports of June 7, 1566). Obviously, however, such documents, without adding anything, confirm information implicit in Vasari's account (1568, vol. VII, p. 530) which was certainly gathered during the Venetian trip of 1566, and in Palladio's "notes" for *I Quattro Libri*. In fragment VI of the BCV. Mss. Cicogna 3617, datable, in agreement with Zorzi (1958, pp. 154-155) between 1561 and 1566, the villa is mentioned.

[68] G. SILVESTRI, *Copie o transunti*, ms. cc. 1225-1226. Concerning the frequency of the disasters and the breaches of the river in the area between 1565 and 1579, there is an interesting and striking documentation in a note by the notary Petrazzolo (ANR. *Antonio Petrazzolo q. Nicolò*: Busta atti 1580-1587: Fascicolo atti and minute January 8, 1580 - September 11, 1581, c. 58 r): "A ciacheduno el quale pernirà alla mano la presente, fatio indubitata fede io Antonio Petrazzuollo nodaro publico de Rovigo et nodaro della villa della Frassinella qualmente l'anno 1565, l'ultima festa de Pasqua, fece una rotta nelli canali a Castelguglielmo la quale affondò detta villa della Frassinella et se perse lo aricolto de quel anno. Item, l'anno 1567, al dì primo novembrio, fece una rotta nell'arger del Po nella villa di Stienta la qual affondò la Frassinella et altri luoghi fino a Rhovigo et se perse lo aricolto de quel anno. Item, l'anno 1576, un giorno delle feste de Pasqua de detto anno fece una ruina de vento tanto grande che batté a terra in la Frassinella molte case, torre e camini et signanter una tezza et camini del clarissimo signor Hieronimo Foscarini quondam clarissimo signor Marcantonio...." The complaints of the Venetian patricians were not just opportunistic. And we can believe Badoer when in 1566 he warns, in regard to the Vespara acreage, that "li quali campi son gravemente sottoposti a le acque piovane et molti di loro non si seminano per esser lochi bassi et sotto posti a le rotte dei canalli et de Po et ogni tratto si rompeno et anegano il tutto et si spende molti dannari in mantenere arzeri ..." (ASV. *X Savi alle Decime: Redecima 1566* b. 135, Condizione n. 297).

[69] See n. 51.

[70] ASV. *Miscellanea Mappe* n. 815. The sheet, made up of many pieces put together but still fragmentary, measures 1930 mm. by 1005 mm. and is inscribed "1549. Valle di San Biasio et Valle Dentro sotto Lendinara." We do not know from what source it came and thus do not know for whom or for what occasion it was drawn; the exactness and ability of the authors come forth clearly.

[71] A. PALLADIO, 1570, L. II, p. 48. The architect points out that the villa was erected "in un sito alquanto rilevato e bagnato da un ramo dell'Adige ove era antiquamente un Castello di Salinguerra da Este cognato di Ezzelino da Romano" and, therefore, he does not state—as some scholars have understood—that traces of the castle (erected by the Bishop of Adria Isacco I in 1104, fortified by Guglielmo Adelardi called Marchesella in 1142, taken by Salinguerra di Torello between 1188 and 1189, and finally destroyed by Azzo d'Este in 1224: G. G. BRONZIERO, 1748, p. 126; G. B. VERCI, 1814, pp. 7 ff.; A. CAPPELLINI, 1941, p. 3) still existed. No signs of it appear in the map of 1549. Moreover, we know that after its destruction in 1224, it was reconstructed as a residence (and used as such by the Pepoli and by others: A. CAPPELLINI, 1941, p. 3), which might be recognized in one of the three houses drawn in the 1549 map.

[72] Cf. B. RIGOBELLO, 1964, pp. 20-24.

[73] See the resumé by RIGOBELLO (1964, pp. 26-37) which draws on the absolutely unquestioned material of the ACL. The original documentation is in the *dossier* of the ASV. *Provveditori sopra Beni Inculti: Processi, Investiture* b. 46, in the file entitled *Lendinara Retratto*, in the part marked *Primo*.

[74] For the history of the magistrature, cf. U. MOZZI, 1927, pp. 17-52; E. CAMPOS, 1937, passim; G. LUZZATTO, 1961, p. 262.

For the identification of the connections with the history of the villa, cf. M. MURARO, 1962, p. 166 (Muraro developed his argument in a 1964 lecture, published in 1966) and G. FIOCCO, 1965, pp. 65 ff.

[75] ASV. *Provveditori sopra Beni Inculti: Processi, Investiture* b. 46, in the file entitled *Lendinara Retratto* and in the part marked *Primo*, cc. 13 r - 15 v and passim. Cf. also B. RIGOBELLO, 1964, p. 28.

[76] See, for a panoramic view, B. RIGOBELLO, 1964, pp. 28-33.

[77] B. RIGOBELLO, 1964, p. 77 (but, obviously, see first the previously cited file in the ASV in the deposit of the *Provveditori sopra Beni Inculti*).

[78] ASV. *Provveditori sopra Camere* B I 10, cc. 45 v - 48 v (instrument of sale of Francesco Badoer of "campi 100" "prativi et pascholivi posti nella Valdentro soto Lendinara," December 16, 1571). The property was quickly declared to the fiscal authorities (ASV. *X Savi alle Decime: Catastici del Dogado e della Terraferma* reg. 450, c. 367 r).

[79] BCV. Mss. PD 2346/VII, on the date, and passim: ACL. *Archivio vecchio di Vespara*, various documents. For a complete chronological register of the documents cf. B. RIGOBELLO, *Origini del Retratto*, ms.

[80] ASV. *Provveditori sopra Beni Inculti: Disegni. Padova e Polesine* pack 28. The great map bears a caption dated March 7, 1557, and signed by Dal Cortivo and by Castaldo, in which, among other things, it is pointed out that "parte del ... dessegno è tratto da altri dissegni fatto per [Dal Cortivo] per ananzi, et parte s'è fatto al presente, de compagnia de misser Iacomo Castaldo cosmograffo"; the exactness of the statement is confirmed by Castaldo in his brief text in which he emphasizes the great care and precision of the drawing (ASV. *Provveditori sopra Beni Inculti: Processi, Investiture* b. 46, in file entitled *Lendinara Retratto*, in the part marked *Primo*, c. 19 r). The original document has remained almost unknown, and the drawing is known only through the ACL. copy taken carefully from the original by Beltrame in 1862, or by the less satisfactory sketch of a detail (the area of the villa) taken from the Lendinara copy by A. C. Bellettato and deposited with the Centro Internazionale di Studi di Architettura "A. Palladio" of Vicenza (*Villa Badoer detta "La Badoera,"* ms.). The reason the document has not yet been traced (undiscovered also by the present writer who contented himself with the kind, but quite inadequate information of Bellettato: 1965-1966, p. 54) is probably due to the inexact information in the caption of the Lendinara copy of the ASV bequest where the "text" should be, in the "archivio del Veneto Magistrato sopra Feudi." The erroneous dating of 1598 of the drawing indicated by F. A. BOCCHI, 1879, pp. 190-191, n. 250, remains inexplicable.

[81] G. G. ZORZI, 1969, p. 98. The late, distinguished scholar does not allude to walls—certainly it cannot have anything to do with the "piedestilo" of which Palladio writes (1570, L. II, p. 48). Nevertheless, it should be emphasized that we should not underestimate the possibility of the presence of a building already existing in 1549 within the newly marked out quadrangle, thus leading us to think that it has to do with, on the contrary, a true and proper enclosing structure which was completed before starting the demolition of the old building and the erection of the new one.

[82] According to ZORZI—who bases himself (1969, p. 98 and fig. 162) on the Bellettato sketch from the Lendinara copy—the "accenno al terrapieno" would indicate that the villa already existed; all the more so since the purposes and the scale of the map, in his judgment, would not have imposed an absolute precision in drawing in the architectural details. Even a rapid examination of the drawing shows, on the contrary, a scrupulous attention to every detail. Think, besides, of the important personalities of Castaldo (cf. R. ALMAGIÀ, 1932)—author, among other things, of a map in 1562 of the Pisani properties in Lonigo (now in the Archivio De Lazara Pisani of Bagnolo)—whose meticulosity has been underlined by DALLA POZZA (1964-1965, pp. 208-209) and admitted by ZORZI himself (1969, p. 55; the sheet is indicated as in the Coll. Mazzadi)—and Dal Cortivo (E. BEVILACQUA, 1970, p. 114).

[83] ASV. *X Savi alle Decime: Redecima* 1537. 116; Condizione added n. 272. The work of architectural renovation or enlargement need not have been of great importance (ASV. *Giudici del Piovego*: Misure b. 21, Quaderno 1539-1559: nothing is recorded).

[84] L. PUPPI, 1965-1966, pp. 63-64; and see here n. 11.

[85] F. BRAUDEL, 1953, pp. 831-844 (and see the "marginal" notes of VENTURA, 1969, pp. 66-67, based on the broad documented panorama offered by the same author, 1964, passim).

[86] R. CESSI, 1936; G. FIOCCO, 1963, and above all, 1965, in particular pp. 66-72 and 82-95 (for the "trattati," earlier published by FIOCCO in 1952, cf. pp. 154-167); cf. M. TAFURI, 1969, p. 122.

[87] M. TAFURI, 1969 (II), pp. 6 ff. and 99. Cf. also, for observations that will be developed, E. FORSSMAN, 1969, pp. 153-154.

[88] For our purposes it is enough to refer back to the pungent comments of M. BARATTO, 1964, pp. 11-68.

[89] L. VENTURI, 1909 (on pp. 105-109 and 140 Venturi provides information about the Cortesi, on the basis of the documentation which we have carefully provided above). Concerning the significance of the Cortesi within the general picture of the theatrical "exploit," see L. PUPPI, 1963, pp. 14-18, L. ZORZI, 1964, and L. PADOAN URBAN, 1966. To underline the "rhetorical" imprint of the various Compagnie della Calza, and especially of the Cortesi, the testimony of Aretino in his letter of November 20, 1540, which is also the last reference of the sources on that association, is valuable. In it (1609 pp. 166 v - 167 r), Aretino rejoices with his correspondent Cesare di Genaro for the "honore che [gli] ha fatto la honorata società de i Cortesi, solo con lo haver[lo] honorevolmente ricevuto nello splendido suo collegio," that "è si grande, che la fama dimostra sommo piacere nel divulgarlo": derived of "vera fratellanza di ... gentil'huomini," so that, "se l'esser servo della nobiltà venetiani, come lo [that is, Aretino], è d'illustre reputazione, cosa è il vedersela compagna nel modo che se la vede il buon Cesare?"

[90] P. PARUTA, 1852 [but II half of the Cinquecento], vol. I, pp. 315-316.

[91] A. VENTURA, 1969, p. 72 (apropos of Agostinetti, 1681).

[92] M. TAFURI, 1969, passim and, in particular, pp. 126-128.

II
THE PROJECT AND ITS EXECUTION

The date of 1557 for the construction of the Villa is based on objective evidence. This date provides a fixed point that dissolves the impasse in the research dealing with the chronology, since (as we have briefly observed and will discuss more fully) the determination of the planning period, for which many discordant answers have been furnished, is obviously postulated on it. In the last chapter we indicated some of the dates that have been advanced, based on considerable but not exhaustive archival research: 1548 for Zorzi; around 1560 for the present writer; 1566 for Burger.[1] Such variations are usual when the determination of a date has been proposed on the basis of a complex nexus of factors but, above all, on the basis of style. Influenced by Burger's conclusions we note a tendency on the part of several specialists to date the Villa in Palladio's late phase: 1565 by Loukomski;[2] 1566 by Wittkower;[3] 1568-70 suggested by Marchiori and seconded by Guiotto and Canova.[4] The hypothesis of a late date remains implicit in those cases where a precise date is prudently avoided; for example, as far back as Banister Fletcher, Heinemann, and Venturi.[5] The suggestion that the date be revised and set back is due to Roberto Pane.[6] The opportuneness of this suggestion is verified by the recent focus on the youth and the early maturity of Palladio's art and by the results of specific analyses by Forssman and Ackerman,[7] who anchor the date at a point before 1560, unlike the radical positions taken by Muraro and Zorzi.[8]

The development of the plans for the Villa must presuppose a careful exploration of the site. This would be in accordance with the strict requirements of the method that Palladio had begun to refine and perfect at the beginning of the 1550s and on whose genesis we will dwell. Forssman—implicitly backed by Cevese on the basis of an exact study of meaningful examples of works[9]—demonstrated that the last lines of the passage entitled "concerning the site to choose for the buildings of the villa" contained in Fragment VI of the Cicogna Manuscript in the Correr Library, reveal an immediate link to the ideas that matured during the time that Palladio joined forces with Daniele Barbaro in the preparation of the 1556 edition of Vitruvius.[10] This fragment provides, in a passage that is left out of the *Quattro Libri*, the sources—Vitruvius and Alberti—of "all those aspects which should be considered in choosing to build a villa." "The duty of the wise architect" appears in the urge to "investigate and search ... with all diligence and effort" the characteristics of the place where he is summoned to work, in order to isolate and select the spot which is most functional in terms of the complex of considerations involved in his work.[11] The project thus springs from the examination of concrete conditions and from the confrontation established among the variable data presented by these conditions: the explicit demands of each individual commission. These concrete conditions, however, were assembled and read as homogeneous representations of various aspects of a class and were obedient to it. The concrete conditions also provide a focus for Palladio's own style, formed through a process of typological experimentation. Even where the relationship with the site is of a "conceptual" order and subordinated (as Tafuri has clearly emphasized) to the exigency of "rendering ... the projection of the type legible,"[12] it remains one of the dialectical poles indispensable to the total undertaking. The description of the "buildings of that magnificent gentleman Francesco Badoer," contained in Fragment VI of the Cicogna Ms. and incorporated into the *Trattato*,[13] implies that there were surveys of the site ("in Polesine, at a place called 'La Frata' on a rather high site, bathed by a branch of the Adige ... Going down then to the plain ..."). It postulates, in short, the immediate connection between the conception and realization, which is a customary part of Palladio's method. From this it is possible to determine that the plans were drawn up and the first phase of the work begun around 1556. This date holds a special significance in Palladio's career due to the appearance of Barbaro's edition of Vitruvius, a book that provided both a summation and a point of departure. We know, as was previously mentioned, that Palladio collaborated on the book with Daniele Barbaro, the Patriarch Elect of Aquilea. This collaboration was acknowledged by Barbaro who states that in the preparation "of the architectural drawings for the important illustrations I used the work of Messer Andrea Palladio, architect of Vicenza, who, of all those whom I have known personally or by hearsay, has, according to the judgment of excellent men, best understood the true meaning of architecture and vastly profited from it, having not only grasped its most beautiful and subtle principles but having also put them into practice, both in his beautiful and exquisite drawings of plans, elevations, and sections and in the execution and erection of many and superb buildings, both in his own country and elsewhere; works which vie with the ancients, which enlighten his contemporaries, and

will arouse the admiration of those yet to come."[14]

Barbaro's words are charged with implications, and it would be advantageous at this point to isolate and analyze them one by one. In the first place, we can verify that Palladio went through a period of training conducted first on the levels of theoretical speculation and then on the levels of experimental and operative demonstrations. After the phase in Vicenza ("in his country") these demonstrations reached other centers of the State and the Capital ("elsewhere"). There was, in other words, a definite casting aside of provincialism in favor of a wide cultural context, as seen in his access to the patronage of the Venetian aristocracy. The supporting external evidence is so varied and clear that there is no need to dwell on the point. It is enough to recall his unsuccessful bid for the post of Director of the *Ufficio del Sale*[15] at the beginning of 1554, or the affair of the petition made in 1555 that he be dismissed as architect for the Loggia of the Basilica in Vicenza.[16] It is more useful to consider the attention paid the Master in Venice, and the circle of relationships and favors he built up there. We find an expression of this in Doni's notation in 1555 that Palladio had written "and designed many and most beautiful works representing all types of buildings; it is a great mistake not to publish them."[17] The judgment is in accord with other statements by Barbaro, such as when he declared in a note in the Vitruvius that he would not go into detail on the subject of habitations, "knowing that a book will be published soon on private houses composed and designed by Palladio, and having seen that nothing is left to desire in that book [he] did not wish to use the effort of others for his own." Instead he reserved for himself the right, in case Vitruvius should be reprinted after Palladio's work had appeared, to draw on "the precepts of that book" based on "admirable

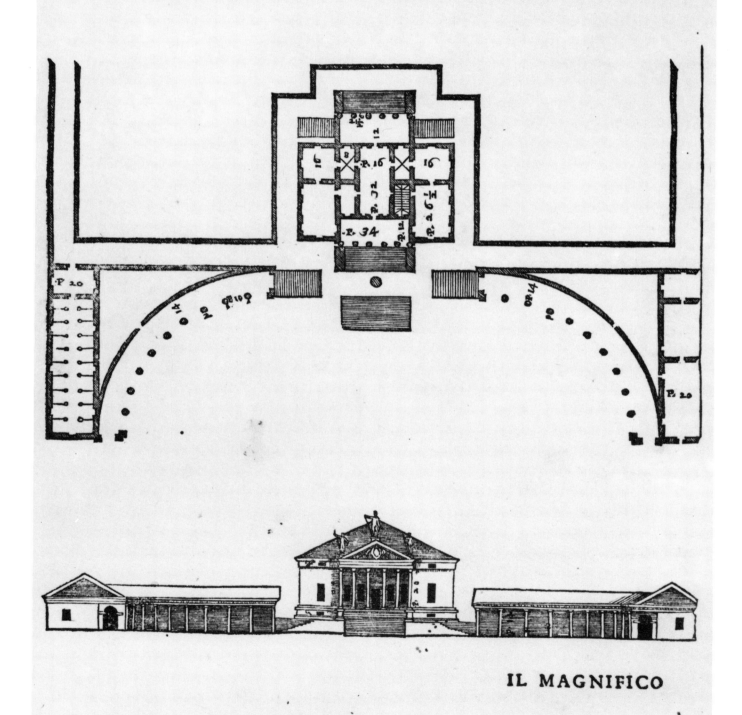

48 · L I B R O

LA SEGVENTE fabrica è del Magnifico Signor Francesco Badoero nel Polesine ad vn luogo detto la Frata, in vn sito alquanto rileuato, e bagnata da un ramo dell'Adige, oue era anticamente vn Castello di Salinguerra da Este cognato di Ezzelino da Romano. Fa basa à tutta la fabrica vn piedestilo alto cinque piedi: à questa altezza è il pauimento delle stanze: lequali tutte sono in solaro, e sono state ornate di Grottesche di bellissima inuentione dal Giallo Fiorentino. Di sopra hanno il granaro, e di sotto la cucina, le cantine, & altri luoghi alla commodità pertinenti: Le colonne delle Loggie della casa del padrone sono Ioniche: La Cornice come corona circonda tutta la casa. Il frontespicio sopra loggie fa vna bellissima uista: perche rende la parte di mezo più eminente de i fianchi. Discendendo poi al piano si ritrouano luoghi da Fattore, Gastaldo, stalle, & altri alla Villa conueneuoli.

IL MAGNIFICO

XII - ANDREA PALLADIO, *Plan and elevation of Villa Badoer.*
From *I Quattro Libri dell'Architettura*, Venice, 1570, II, XIII, p. 48.

knowledge of building" and clarifying "all that pertains to the building of private edifices, with the plans, sections and elevations of everything, and palaces that he has designed for various nobles."[18] Since "little by little a grander and more magnificent Architecture will show itself in its ancient form and beauty," on the basis of what Palladio has done, and on the condition— here Barbaro exclaims "if I can pray, I pray and pray again ..."—that "the people of [his] country ... may remember that lacking neither wealth nor power to have honored works, need to provide what they lack in genius and knowledge. This will happen when they become convinced that they do not know what in fact they do not know, and what cannot be known without training, effort, and knowledge. And if they think that the traditional practice must be the best they deceive themselves greatly, because it is in fact highly defective and is bad usage."[19] The imperative for a "new usage" destined to bring about "the true elegance and beauty of the ancients," in a form amenable to the postulates of "decorum" urged by the new "aristocratic" order of the Venetian ruling class, is stated with extreme clarity within the context of the ideology that represents, on the superstructural level—the level of self-awareness—these structural changes which have been outlined in the preceding chapter. Barbaro in his discussion of Palladio, more specifically in his affirmation of an identity with Palladio's aims, attests to an exchange of views, a discussion, and finally a rich and close association which Forssman correctly places at the time of the Patriarch Elect's return from his ambassadorship in England, i.e., in 1550, which is, not by chance, the year of Trissino's death. Forssman sees the association as based on a new reading of the Vitruvian "bible," strengthened in 1554 by the trip,[20] recorded by Gualdo, to Rome for "the fifth time, with

several of his Venetian friends," with Barbaro in first place among them.[21] Credit is also due Forssman for having insisted on the special nature of this trip in respect to the earlier ones, which lies in its overwhelming commitment to create in an accurate typological structure, obedient to functional and practical imperatives, the "house of the ancients" described by Vitruvius, though that description was ambiguous and lacking in demonstrable archaeological substantiation.[22]

It seems to me that from a point of view such as this, one may note a polarization of Palladio's interests in a pattern emphasizing love of learning and of experimentation—a pattern that can be attributed to the bond established with the enlarged circle of his patronage. "I was not content," Palladio wrote in *L'antichità di Roma* published in Rome in 1554, "with that alone [i.e., with the many conscientious authors, both ancient and modern]" "I also wanted to see all of it and measure it precisely with my own hands." Along with his investigation of the antique remains, he did not fail to mention visits "to the Palace of the Pope and the Belvedere."[23] It is also easy to imagine that he was prompted to investigate works by Vignola and Ligorio;[24] an encounter of those works with Barbaro has been hypothesized by Zorzi.[25] This sort of thing is a reflection of Palladio's long and eventually productive restlessness and of his desire to come to grips with the new modern answers, to check their validity in relation to his own vexing problems. In regard to the question of the country house (though Tafuri has correctly stated that it is unwise to make a sharp division in regard to planning methods between the house in the city and the house in the country[26]), scholars have pointed out that the predominant tendency in Palladio's work up to the 1540s was an abstract exercise. Such an exercise was aimed at defining a model

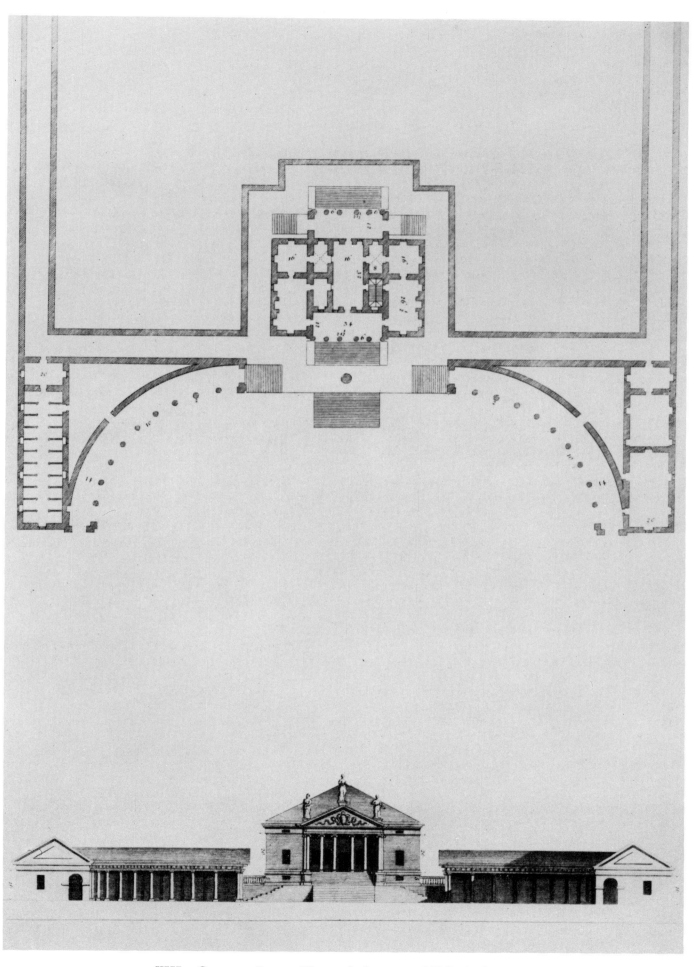

XIII - GIACOMO LEONI, *Plan and elevation of Villa Badoer.*
From *The Architecture of A. Palladio in four Books...*, London, 1721, II, pl. XXXIII.

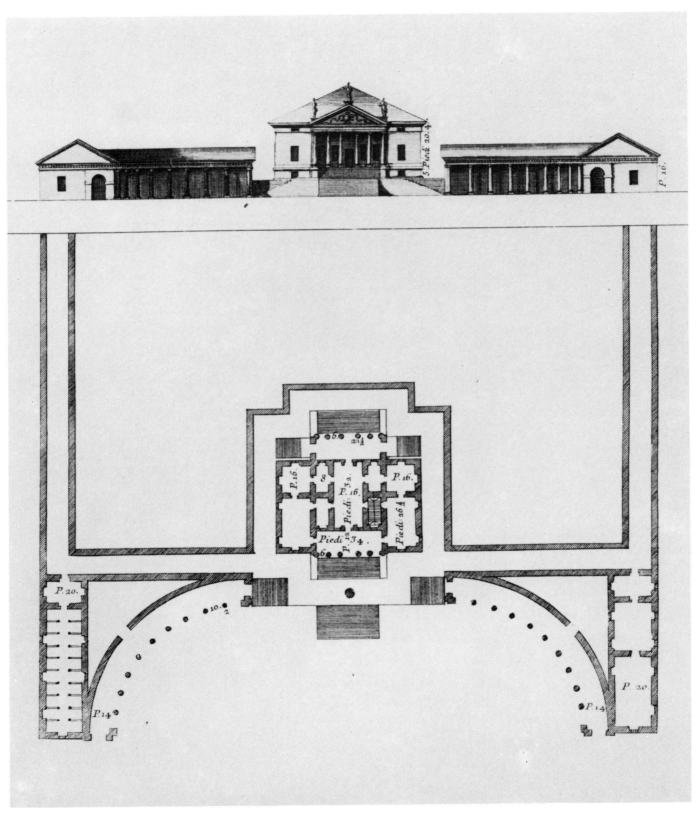

XIV - FRANCESCO MUTTONI, *Elevation and plan of Villa Badoer.*
From *Architettura di Andrea Palladio Vicentino*, Venice, V, 1744, II, pl. XXXII.

which would contain in its planimetric arrangement spaces organized in relation to the central hall and in its elevations the articulation of a classically defined façade.[27] The concrete experimentation that occupied the following decade reveals a deepening of these investigations, and that in turn is translated into his works. He was at the same time spurred on by the ideas he received during the course of his trips to Rome, by the stimulation that came from his meetings with Serlio and Cornaro, and by experiencing the parallel works carried out by Giulio Romano, Falconetto, Sansovino, and Sanmicheli.[28] On the level of dynamic thrust and counterthrust that influenced his work, he was, above all, stimulated by the needs of his patrons in Vicenza and the provinces, patrons who, insofar as their class was concerned, were persons whose economic basis was in the land and whose ideological consciousness was aristocratic and feudal. This meant a change of function and form in the villa and carried with it the need for a renewal of the traditional repertory of types[29] and the development of a stylistic instrument able to sustain it and to establish it. Thus there came into being a cultural operation that was retardataire in the sense that it retraced the ground already traveled and was discounted by the classicizing circles in Rome that gravitated around Bramante. It also involved salvaging the main lines of the Venetian tradition— the *Magie der Darstellungkünste*. It aimed at a "decisive chromatic achievement," which overcame the risk that it might harden into something academic.[30] The interplay between the large scale of the service areas and the monumentality of the villa proper, equally respondent to both structural and superstructural needs, urgently required, in the meantime, consolidation with the context of a well integrated classical vocabulary. This posed the most serious and difficult problem for Palladio.[31] It would be out of place here to spend time on the cultural conditions which led the architect to confront, lay out, and develop the historical task given him in this or that phase of a coherent process, discarding on the grounds of a strict classicistic choice the abstract treatise-oriented positions characteristic of the Vicentine intellectual circles that gravitated around Trissino, restoring the ferment of the Venetian bourgeois tradition. It is this tradition, so very vital and rich in terms of future developments, which permanently conditioned the course of all future inquiry. Upon reaching its proper aesthetic level, with all its characteristic and necessary implications, from the manipulation of style to the ordering of the forms, the tradition expressed itself in a creative design which was to have an autonomous life and an incomparable destiny.[32]

The concern here is to note the key moment around 1550 (perceptively indicated by Wittkower and subtly interpreted by Rosci) in the planimetric study of the body of the residence through the preparation of a geometric scheme centering on the fixed point of an axis of penetration that runs from the front to the back. This axis, by freeing the atrium of obligatory Vitruvian inspirations—centrality and symmetry—established it as the basic module of the central block with "the rooms measured off ... in two parallel rows." In such a way we observe a freer, more open interpretation of the atrium referred to by Vitruvius and tried, for example, in Villa Thiene at Quinto. Palladio's inspiration came from a reworking of the Venetian longitudinal central hall[33] which he opened up and placed in a conceptual formula that permitted an unlimited range of types and styles. This he did without departing from the principle inherent in his way of thinking. He constructed his formula on the rules of the correct proper alignment wherein the formal arrangement had to follow the functional forces in their complexity and in their variability. Consequently, the formula was not an immobile and crystallized modular paradigm, but a dynamic, refined, well organized instrument of intervention.[34] An analogous procedure occurred at about the same chronological juncture. In the front elevation is seen an adoption of the pronaos with a pediment that enhances and sets off the façade. This motif, which derives from the Roman temple, finally resolves the Vitruvian ambiguities and the lack of archaeological evidence of secular architecture, as well as the unsatisfactory nature of the loggia solution suggested by Cornaro.[35] On the basis of these developments, which had already been codified in the tabulation made by Barbaro, there is, as Tafuri states,[36] an inevitable de-historicization and de-symbolization of the data on which the scholarly processes are focused. But this development does not constitute a reduction of the data to a state of neutrality that permits the most casual manipulations. Rather it is a stage in a process which transposed the original symbolical concepts and integrated them into a new synthesis:[37] the consecration of the architectonic expression of the ideology of "living on the land." "I have built," Palladio wrote in his *Quattro Libri*,[38] "in all the villas and also in some of the city houses a frontispiece on the forward façade where the principal doors are placed, because such frontispieces show the entrance of the house and add very much to the grandeur and magnificence of the work, the front being thus made more eminent than the other parts. Besides, they prove to be especially useful for the builder's coats of arms, which usually are put in the middle of façades. The ancients also used them in their buildings, as may be seen in the remains of temples and other public edifices ... ."

More difficult, however, was the problem of the symbolic relationship of the central block to the service areas. This problem seems to have already been given attention in the drawings of the Temple of Hercules at Tivoli. We see this especially in the RIBA folios IX, 8 (fig. VI), where attention is given to the planimetric connections, and in RIBA IX, 7 (fig. VIII). In this last he turns his attention to ways of linking the pronaos and the arcades. Herein we see a distant awareness[39] that will become much clearer during the 1550s and that will find its most ambitious translation in the acropolis-like plan of Villa Trissino at Meledo, which was flawed in the execution by an abstract procedure, especially insofar as the grandeur of the symbols are concerned.[40] What must be observed is that the accentuation of his research, the direction of his prospects, and finally his connotations coincide increasingly with his close relationship with Barbaro— with the friendship that grew from it and with the establishment of a partnership the main point of which was the commitment to visit once more both Vitruvius and Rome. We may properly conjecture that the establishment of the partnership implied the restoration of a type of patronage that was rich in significance and historically identifiable. In the passage quoted from Fragment VI of the Cicogna MS., which Forssmann used as evidence of Palladio's close association with Barbaro, Palladio identifies the patron of a villa as a "gentleman of great splendor and advantage." It is a transparent description of a member of the new Venetian aristocracy ("great gentlemen of the Republic" he states in Fragment V of the same manuscript). The principal reasons for commissioning villas are indicated in the terms "utility and consolation," or "to see and embellish his possessions and to increase his facilities with industry and the arts of agriculture." Life in a villa served, through physical exercise, to preserve "health and robustness," to offer to the "spirit fatigued by the turmoil of the town ... much restoration and consolation," and to afford the opportunity "quietly...to attend to the study of literature and contemplation. For this reason the wise men of antiquity often used to retire to similar places where, visited by virtuous friends and relatives, having country properties, gardens, fountains, and similar pleasant places and [having] above all their virtue..., were easily able to follow a life as blessed as one may obtain here below." Life in the villa therefore "is made up principally of family and personal affairs"[41] so that such "great gentlemen, mainly of the Republic, will require houses with loggias, and spacious well-decorated rooms." The synthesis between the economic function and "recreation," in an elevated sense of the term, is supplied by the site (with Palladio consequently assigning great importance to the surveying) as we have noted at the beginning of this chapter. The agricultural land is thus urbanized and ennobled in the classical manner. This comes about through the commitment of the Venetian nobility to the country. A commitment, as it is a reflection of private initiative, goes in tandem with the commitment to a land reorganization as a public duty entrusted by the State to Sanmicheli.[42] In other words, the process of urbanization is one in which, according to Zevi's fine analysis, the Palladian method challenges the isolation of the villa by a type of intervention which grounds the architectural complex in nature and extends out into it, engaging and absorbing the most subtle topographical stimulae from it and enhancing these aspects through the characteristic openness of its form.[43] Still the most urgent problem of a spatial composition affected by such demands always ends by concentrating on the "two kinds of buildings" which, differentiated by function, "require for the villa one [place] for the living quarters of the landlord and his family, the other for looking after the housing, the income, and the animals of the villa." "The site must be divided" on this basis.[44] As emphasized by Barbaro, "these villas must provide much commodity, and must seek much commodity from nature...They must be constructed in such a way that the building is not lacking in land nor the land in buildings."[45] The solution that Palladio pursued in the broad reaches of his own imagination and in the concrete world of facts obviously did not aim to establish a fixed and immobile model —something that never happens. Rather his aim was to establish a highly articulate method capable of realizing, in confrontation with the site, the total process implicit in this type of urbanization. The genesis of the plan of the villa for Leonardo Mocenigo on the Brenta is, in terms of the development of this process, more directed, more symptomatic, and more exemplary of the future (which in any case remains inaccessible to us) than the coeval Villa Angaran in Angarano which, even so, is to be considered as an important moment of the phase to which ideas for the Villa Badoer belong. Zorzi has most probably determined the correct chronological sequence of the four drawings referring to Villa Mocenigo that are in the Royal Institute of British Architects Collection in London. To each of these sheets, moreover, Zorzi devotes a scholarly examination to which it would be futile to return.[46] It seems also that Zorzi's chronology, which recalls that proposed by Gallo, is in general acceptable, though it is necessary to focus it within a context closely aligned to ideas for Villa Badoer.[47] For our purposes it is useful to observe the transition from the first formulation of the idea, represented by RIBA XVI, 2 (fig. VII), which is based on a solution of the front façade of the central block, worked out, as Wittkower correctly affirmed, around 1550. This solution is characterized by a central penetrating axis with lateral wings and an arcaded service block based on the brilliant example of the Villa dei Vescovi at Luvi-gliamo.[48] The intermediary phase is repre-sented by RIBA XVI, 1, which, without modifying the order of the main façade, shows traces of a renewal of Vitruvian in-fluences, transmitted—indirectly perhaps —through Trissino's description of the Pal-ace of Areta ("a fine court, enclosed by four loggias") and expressed in the central peri-style.[49]

Finally we arrive at the restless version of RIBA V, 1 v (fig. IX). The most interest-ing aspect in this plan is not that the concept was developed by means of exten-sive use of an archaeological vocabulary extrapolated from an archaeological reper-tory or that it was the endeavor to open up the central block, a move which is based on nostalgia for the atriums of Vitruvius's "villa of the ancients." Its greatest interest lies in the *pentimenti* which provides traces of the development of the front portico, both curvilear and rectilinear. Thus we note signs of a hypothesis, barely suggested and very summarily formulated, which will re-main the fixed point of departure in rela-tion to the situations to be faced, although modified by the formation of the encompass-ing space and in accordance with the desire to enhance the dwelling within the environ-ment.[50] Meanwhile, in the plan of the build-ing is a resolution of the interplay between the two constitutive elements of the villa, whose interrelationships must be incorpo-rated into the composition in accordance with the symbolic and figurative significance of the orders. The evidence of a *virage* or "bending" (beginning with his studies for Villa Madama and expressed in the draw-ing RIBA X, 18 [fig. X]) seems patent and illuminating and, according to Gloton, may be considered Palladio's reply to those examples by Vignola and Ligorio which he studied in Rome during a trip there in 1554.[51] The final solution of the difficult problem seen in folio RIBA X, 2r (fig. XI),

and, with variation, in the plate in the *Quattro Libri*, provides an architectonic or-ganization of the cultivated land.[52] In this solution preference is given to the curvi-linear layout. It seems evident that the form was taken from studies of the Roman the-atre,[53] from which is derived the joining of the colonnade with the pronaos of the cen-tral block, the elevation of the entrance stairway, and the union of the entrance stairway with the functional structures, that is, with the long colonnaded barns. These same problems occurred in placing the con-cept of the Villa di Fratta on the site (figs. XXXII, XXXIV, XXXIX-XL). Al-though in the definitive version all preoccu-pation with basing the central block on the peristyle plan is discarded and the problem is resolved by a building without an inner court, we could not remove only the last sheet considered from Francesco Badoer's project and nothing more. The design published in 1570 (fig. XII) reveals, in rela-tion to the building as executed, variations which a reading of the accompanying cap-tions makes clear. In fact, Palladio wrote: "The whole construction stands of a five foot high podium: in this level are the ground-floor rooms that are all flat ceilinged ... . Above these rooms are the granaries and under them the kitchen, the cellars, and other household conveniences. The columns of the loggias on the principal part of the house are Ionic. The cornice encircles the whole house like a crown. The frontispiece over the loggias is a lovely sight because it makes the entrance in the center stand out from the sides. Going down to the ground level one comes to the Land Agent's and the Farmer's lodgings, the cow sheds, and other conveniences of country life."[54] We observe —and Zorzi's analysis on this proposition remains accurate[55]—that modification had been made in the system of embankments, or earthfills and walls, that elevates the site reserved for the owner's house and provides

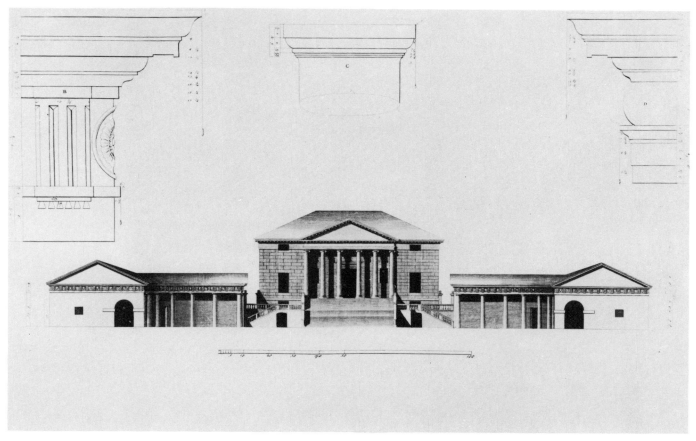

XV - OTTAVIO BERTOTTI SCAMOZZI, *Elevation of Villa Badoer.*
From *Le Fabbriche e i disegni di Andrea Palladio*, Vicenza, III, 1781, pl. XLII.

the base for further elevation created by the podium (scale drawings VIII, X). The stairs, in fact, reach the level of the embankment by means of two flights each of a different height and treatment (plates 12-13), separated from one another by a landing, where we see the well head which was later removed and placed in the garden (fig. L), and widening out onto a second landing extending beyond the area of the loggia (plate 30). The third flight of stairs rises above the level of the podium and comes out in the pronaos or portico (plate 31). The stairs which, starting from the second level, lead down into the curvilinear colonnades are reduced to the width of the arcades into which they descend (plates 24-25, 29). The entire system is furnished with balustrades (plates 28, 31-34). Moreover, the *barchesse* or colonnaded barns continue beyond the limits of the hemicycles (plates 14-15),

which are made up of only six intercolumniations (plates 16-19, 21), and extend out to join the enclosing wall in front. The façade toward the open country has neither a loggia nor flights of stairs. Finally, the roof is lowered in relation to the pediment which remains without statues (color plate *a*, and plates 4-5). We note that apart from minor differences in the measurements,[56] the distribution of the rooms in the plan of the *piano nobile* of the owner's house corresponds substantially to the division between the service areas of cellars and basements and the "granary" (scale drawings II, IV). It must be mentioned briefly that the building as it now stands corresponds in great measure to the original project. Above all, on the basis of the general principles provided by the illustrations in the *Quattro Libri*, we see the results of the rethinking and the re-elaborations brought into play by

XVI - OTTAVIO BERTOTTI SCAMOZZI, *Cross section of Villa Badoer.*
From *Le Fabbriche e i disegni di Andrea Palladio*, Vicenza, III, 1781, pl. XLIII.

the didactic needs of the *Trattato*. Those illustrations, in other words, represent the consequences of a process of abstraction and idealization executed graphically to answer specific needs. In this respect we may cautiously admit that in the preparation of the engravings of 1570 there was an attempt to restore the original design of the building which had been vitiated or changed by unexpected events such as environmental considerations, inadequacies and deficiencies of the workmen, or pressures from the patron.[57] "I know very well," Palladio wrote in Fragment V of the Cicogna MS., "that the architect finds it more necessary to accommodate himself to the will of those who provide the money, than to that which ought to be respected."[58] However, the care and attention he gave, even if from a distance, to those undertakings for which he had responsibility is very evident.[59]

We know nothing about the presence of the Master in the project at Fratta. He must have been there at least during the preliminary phase to examine the site, but there may have been no other trip, since Cevese's[60] penetrating observations persuade us that the construction was contracted to and directed by local masons, who if not awkward and devoid of skill were of modest competency.[61] Although their abilities were inadequate to translate into material form the richness of Palladio's ideas (figs. XXVIII-XXX), they were also incapable of manipulating and betraying the plans that were given them. We note at once that the back loggia and flight of stairs were never built (scale drawing VI). In their place was a way of windows that overlooked a small terrace, traces of which are still quite plain at the level of the *piano nobile* (plates 36-37) and are, in any case, visible in the Ber-

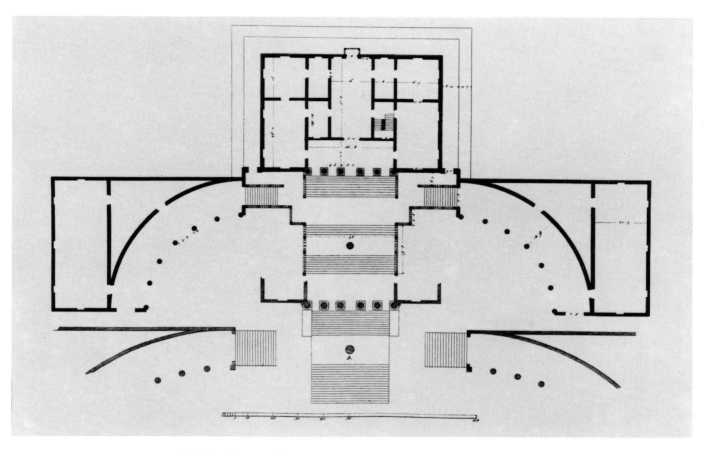

XVII - Ottavio Bertotti Scamozzi, *Plan of Villa Badoer.*
From *Le Fabbriche e i disegni di Andrea Palladio*, Vicenza, III, 1781, pl. XLIV.

totti Scamozzi plans (figs. XVI-XVII) where it is shown to have had a balustrade. Therefore, it may be hypothesized that the omission of the ceremonial features from the back façade had been decided by the patron, who must have thought them unnecessary in confrontation with the empty expanse of open countryside and with the short extent of his property (the acreage in Bragola), which on that side (fig. XXXIII) was partly occupied by the cultivated fields and by the garden (plates 39, 41). These considerations must have prompted Badoer to ask the architect for an imperious and more varied development of the entranceway at the front (plates 2-3), a necessary ingredient of which would have been the adoption of a prominent balustrade (figs. XXXV-XXXVI and scale drawing XIIc), absent from the illustration published in 1570.[62] The lowering of the roof is also consistent with the

intention of throwing into relief, and giving greater emphasis to, the frontispiece, the field of which would have originally contained the escutcheon, the arms of the Badoer-Loredan alliance, the heraldic record of friendship and kinship.[63] In addition, this frontispiece is slightly but noticeably brought forward (plate 11) from the Ionic hexastyle (plate 6) of the loggia. A little later the same treatment is carried out in Villa Foscari alla Malcontenta. In short, the temple front determined the appearance of the whole façade and gives visual expression to the profound motivations of the patronage. Its aristocratic and feudal significance is stated by the caption of the illustration in its allusion to the cornice "that encircles the whole house like a crown." It is unnecessary to mention the awareness, also expressed in the caption, of the determinate role assigned to the loggia (plates 7-9). The changes that are found in the arrangement of the landfills and the retaining walls (plate 35), no doubt due to decisions made during the building process, remain hard to explain, although it may be permissible to link them to practical functional criteria.[64] The same is not true of the blatant changes in the arrangement of the wings—changes that were made in a very late phase, violating the solution prepared by Palladio and corresponding, in respect to the development of the wings, to the illustration published in 1570. The wings are modified only in the reduction of the colonnade and in the breadth of its curvature. For the purposes of reliable documentation the illustrations in Bertotti Scamozzi are more useful than those plates in later editions of the *Trattato* of the 17th and 18th centuries, which do no more than reproduce a substantial transcription of the illustration published in the original edition repeating word for word the comment about them. The edition by Leoni (fig. XIII) transcribes the text with some slight inaccuracies.[65] The Ware edition, however, inverts the placement of the stables and, in the house proper, inverts the position of the stairs that lead from the *piano nobile* to the "granary."[66] The edition by Mucci restricts itself to removing, perhaps on the suggestion of the plan by Bertotti Scamozzi, the roof pinnacle and the ceremonial aspects of the back façade.[67] The illustration by Muttoni (fig. XIV) follows the Palladian engraving with complete accuracy, but the caption, details of which show he inspected the building himself, states that the building was "finished as Palladio himself illustrated it."[68] The annotation is thus ambiguous and ambivalent. To overcome the impasse it is necessary to turn to Bertotti Scamozzi who provides extremely careful measurements and observations.[69] He testifies to the presence of "two semicircular colonnades (plates 26-27) which flank [the owner's house]; behind these colonnades,

in accordance with Palladio's designs, should be the stables and other places which have been put to different uses, perhaps in accordance with the ideas of those who later owned the house."[70] The illustration of the elevations (figs. XV-XVI) and the plans (fig. XVII) show the reduction in the development of the portico, which apparently took place in the building phase. The part of the portico that projects forward was reduced from ten columns to six. The columns were separated by briefer intercolumniations, 7.8 feet instead of 10 feet, and the portico was reduced in depth from 14 feet to 12.9 feet. At the same time, the illustrations verify the correspondence of the lateral barns with the starting point of the curves of the portico (figs. XXXII, XXXIV), joined in perspective by the tympanum. The width of the two wings is the same as Palladio indicated in the *Quattro Libri*, 20.3 feet and 20 feet; but they are stripped of the function prescribed by Palladio (there are no "stables" in the left wing), and several variations in the opening of windows and other passages are evident. Moreover, the adjustment of the wings to different uses must already have taken place before 1676, at which time it seems the two buildings (or only one?) were converted into guest quarters.[71] As we shall see in the next chapter, the reason for this conversion was the need to reorganize and expand the complex into a working farm without interfering with the equilibrium of the component parts of the outer wings. The wings remain intact and are only altered, in respect to the design of 1570, in terms of the size, the internal proportions, and the size of the whole in comparison with the main block, again for the purpose of enhancing it. This is a result of a more sober and restrictive treatment of the outline—a treatment that is not disproportionate and, consequently, not intrusive and dispersive of the concentration

XVIII - ANDREA PALLADIO, *Sketches of the so-called Villa of Maecenas at Tivoli.*
London, RIBA, IX, 13 v.

of effect of the grandiose presence (plates 20, 22-23). The late date of the elongation of the wings is confirmed by Temanza's statement [72] and by two eighteenth century maps. We also find proof in the impertinent, formal incongruity of that thick annex, which can be explained by new, impelling functional necessities. One of the maps, dated August 19, 1757, and which is exclusively planimetric and quite inaccurate (fig. XXIII), causes some perplexity.[73] The other dated 1775, is much more accurate (fig. XXIV), even though the columnar wings seem to be extended down to the street and are shown in the same manner as in the Bertotti Scamozzi illustration—joined to an ambulatory with six intercolumniations.[74] For the sake of completeness, it can be stated that a direct examination of the

outer walls of the wings clearly reveals the line of jointure between the service areas planned and constructed by Palladio and the extensions. However it is more difficult to pinpoint the joining line on the inside wall and on the walls facing the courtyard.[75] The engraving of 1570 does not include a drawing of the division between the street and "the piazza in front of" the villa, which, according to Temanza, during his time "came out in a halfcircle." [76] However, it coincided with the enclosing wall of brick in front, a wall that can be related to the original location (scale drawings XIa, XIIb) and therefore to Palladio's project (plates 38, 40). The colonnades and service areas together with the pedimented façade must have been united to the present enclosing wall by stretches of wall of the same design (which would have contained in the severely stylized rhythmns a recollection of castle motifs [77]), thus placing in the foreground a quadrilateral embankment of the open space. It is a theme that is restated in the walled area in back (scale drawing XIb) set aside for the most private areas of cultivation like a garden, an indispensable ingredient. We need only think of Doni's rhetoric about the pleasure of the signore.[78] These find reflection, for example, in Palladio's sketches for Villa Mocenigo and in explicit statements like "the gardens, the cultivated areas, which are the spirit and pleasure of the villa." Moreover, we must also attribute to Palladio the opening at the center of the back enclosing wall (plate 39). This opening is on an axis that runs through the entrance, across the loggia and central hall of the main block (plates 4-5, 45), and faces the open countryside—the gardens, the orchards and the wide spread of the fields, and the noble statement of the two small aedicules (figs. XXXVII-XXXVIII) inspired by studies of the so-called Villa of Maecenas at Tivoli (fig. XVIII) in folio RIBA IV, 13 v.[79]

Now that the project has been restored to its true outlines, the illustration drawn *a posteriori* for the *Quattro Libri* is, in comparison, "more regulated and easier" because of the book's manual-like purpose. Thanks to the arduous interpretive program, the Villa is now freed of the incrustations of time, and the autograph structure has been recovered. Villa Badoer proves to be one of the most coherent and sublime of the works by Palladio within the stylistic period that centers on the middle of the 1550s. Here the ideological motives of the patronage (patronage being understood as the individual patron operating within a nexus of homogeneous tendencies) are changed and resolved within the free universe of the expressive, stylistic, and cultural motives of the architect, who exalts them

by placing them in a creation of ordered perfection. Or, to put it another way, the imaginary universe of the Master (identifiable in the intrepid dream of the complete restoration of classicism) comes in contact with the vocation (stripped of any autobiographical connotation) of a class that strives to illustrate in self-glorifying terms its own aristocratic status by constructing an edifice that is, at the same time, responsive to the economic and structural exigencies underlying its consciousness. All these elements are fused in an incomparable formal event: the *Monumentalpalast*. This is something which grew out of a complex of experiments in which each level of functionality was consolidated and transmitted, not something worked out in advance and transmitted with indifference.[80] "Commodity," the architect wrote,[81] "means that house which will be suitable to the standing of the person who will inhabit it, and its parts will correspond to one another and to the whole." This principle is among the most vital points of departure of the development of Venetian culture that influenced Palladio. It appears in the work of Alvise Cornaro, according to whom "the perfectly commodious building" is to be given preference over the "very beautiful but incommodious one." This principle is also strictly linked to and balanced with the principle of "decorum."[82] "We will also preserve Decorum in regard to the work," Palladio specifies, "if the parts will comply with the whole."[83] By placing this statement in relation to the preceding one, we throw light on the characteristics implied by the design and the execution of Villa Badoer. The typological choice, far from being worked out intellectually in an abstract process, has to originate (as Villa Badoer originated), from those concrete manifestations in which the general concept of the patron is particularized and has to be validated by the syntactic instrumentation of a classicistic vocabulary. From Palladio's point of view this presupposes, in accordance with the method considered above, the stripping away of the original historical meanings and the restoration and revitalization of the structure of the style. Thus, the arrangement of the colonnades incorporates and transposes the service buildings into the rhythmic cadences of the Tuscan Order, which gives visual expression to an unambiguous network of meanings. The wings curve and move inward toward the main block with its Ionic frontispiece. The frontispiece, in its turn, frees itself and presses outward to present its own network of meanings which—with the "import of immediate decoration" and by the affirmation of clear scenographic overtones—frees itself from the homage which the purist pays to the canons, these being varied at will (plates 14-15).

The construction and the definition of a typological organism takes shape and comes to life, by means of stylistic modulations, in an ever changing dialectic of images. It is a dialectic which transcends the images, returns to them, and is absorbed in them to become the fundamental moment of the articulation of the space as the "animating organ."[84] The long and pause-filled stairway, rich in its complexity and discovered through tireless investigations, is the coherent connection between the components of the farm and the mansion of the owner. It is the stairs that provide guideposts and channel the atmospheric circulation of the court (scale drawings XIV-XV). They direct the movement along the optical axis, inaugurated by the entranceway that looks toward the river ("a beautiful and a most convenient thing"), and project it outward toward the open country, which will yet remain unaffected in its growth by the dominion of such an unfamiliar and inflexible form— a form that is detached from an urbanization extraneous either to its past or its future. The movement generated by the stairs transverses the loggia and the atrium (scale drawing XIIIa) and extends, through the elegant doorway (plate 44), into the area of the cultivated fields and from there into the open countryside.[85] But it is the atrium that divides and formulates the meter that was prepared (at the conclusion of Palladio's then recent review of Vitruvius) for this particular situation, through the development of the plans and elevations, for the functions of the residence of the owner within the nexus of spatial articulations that extend the external rhythms (scale drawings I-II). An immutable sequence of conjunctions extends from the arrangement of the large and small room of the *piano nobile*, which is regulated solely by its own intimate logic, to the "granary" and connected by the same flights of stairs to the area of the magnificent "basements" (figs. XLI-XLVI), which also leads outside. Finally, according to the illuminating interpretation of Argan[86] (used in an anticlassical sense so as to deny in its concrete application the syntactical use of a vocabulary obedient to classicism[87]), the "nonperspective dynamics" are conditioned by the quality of the natural site selected while, at the same time, controlled by it (plate 1 and scale drawing I). Thus, they forever create the site in the form of a magic and lyrical equilibrium of movements that animate and focus upon a new "classicism" that is unaware of explicit crises and wounds, unconscious of doubts, and joyful and contented in its own certainty.

NOTES TO CHAPTER II

[1] See in Ch. I, nn. 61-63 for the references.

[2] G. K. LOUKOMSKI, 1927, p. 86, cf. also, G. K. LOUKOMSKI, 1926, vol. I, pp. 10-11.

[3] R. WITTKOWER, 1962, p. 74.

[4] G. MARCHIORI, 1954, pp. 447-448 (and cf. G. MAZZOTTI, 1963, p. 136); M. GUIOTTO, 1964, pp. 76-78; A. CANOVA, 1970, pp. 33-37. Recently also L. GRASSI (1966, p. 32 of the index) confirms the 1568-1570 chronology, referring it however to the construction and stating that the planning was "certainly before that."

[5] F. BANISTER FLETCHER, 1902, pp. 64-65; W. HEINEMANN, 1909, pp. 61-62; A. VENTURI, 1940, pp. 465-468 (singularly, the scholar turns the Scortico stream into the Adige river, p. 465). The position of others such as GURLITT, 1914, G. M. CANTACUZÈNE, 1928, A. MELANI, 1928, etc., is analogous. Recently, IVANOFF (1967, in particular pp. 62-166) does not express a precise chronology.

[6] R. PANE, 1961, p. 276.

[7] E. FORSSMAN, 1965, pp. 67-68 (recently Forssman has tended to move the date back to around 1553; E. FORSSMAN, 1969, p. 154); J. S. ACKERMAN, 1966, p. 14 and 1967, pp. 47-49.

[8] M. MURARO, 1954, p. 107; G. G. ZORZI, 1969, p. 98.

[9] E. FORSSMAN, 1969, pp. 152-153; R. CEVESE, 1969.

[10] Without entering into the merits of the authorship of the version, the transcription of the Cicognara Manuscript by G. G. ZORZI, has been utilized: cf. now p. 184.

[11] G.G. ZORZI, 1958, p. 184.

[12] For the complete discussion see M. TAFURI, 1969, pp. 125-126 (and for a characterization of the procedural method, p. 135, n. 11).

[13] G. G. ZORZI, 1958, p. 187 and A. PALLADIO, 1570, L. II, p. 48.

[14] D. BARBARO, 1556, p. 40.

[15] G. B. LORENZI, 1868, p. 281 (document 601, republished by ZORZI, 1965, p. 137).

[16] The reference is in L. FERRARI, 1880, p. 14. For the suspension of payments to Palladio in 1560 because of his frequent absences from Vicenza, see A. MAGRINI (1845, p. 81) and the comments of BARBIERI (1964, p. 59). It should also be noted that according to the aforecited LORENZI (1868, p. 287, document 615; also studied and republished by ZORZI, 1965, p. 137) Palladio entered his own plan in the competition for the commission for the "scala d'oro" for the Ducal Palace. On the relationship between the architect and Venice, see the specific studies by GALLO (1955 and 1956, passim) and, more thoroughly, ZORZI (1960, in particular pp. 108-109; and 1965, pp. 130-137).

[17] A. F. DONI, 1555, p. 155.

[18] D. BARBARO, 1556, p. 279 [sic! but rather 178)].

[19] Ibid. The statement, like the preceding one, is repeated in the successive editions in Italian; 1567, p. 303 (and p. 64). An organic study of the "intellectual" Barbaro remains to be done, although the Elogio of Diedo (1817) remains informative for an overall view. It would be useful to have a study that would clarify the scientific exigencies in relationship with the Aristotelian culture (see n. 21 below); that aspect is not treated in the fine study by P. PASCHINI (1962) which is more concerned with Barbaro as an ecclesiastic than a man of culture.

[20] See, on this point, above all E. FORSSMAN, 1962, p. 33 and 1966, pp. 75-76; also G. G. ZORZI, 1969, pp. 169-170.

[21] P. GUALDO, 1617, p. 93. Although the name of Barbaro is not given by the biographer, doubts about the Patriarch Elect's presence would be out of place. His presence is, moreover, acknowledged by all the specialists. In any case it suffices to refer to the succinct reasoning of ZORZI, 1958, pp. 21-23. The acute observation of TAFURI (1969, p. 124), relative to the contacts established at a certain point by Palladio with circles open to a civil use of scientific progress—circles rich in future prospects for the methodology of planned undertakings—can, in a fitting way, be placed in conjunction with the circumstances to which we refer, converging to increase the implications of Palladio's turn toward Venice. Consequently, the names pronounced by Tafuri of Marcantonio Barbaro (see C. YRIARTE, 1874, passim) and of Giacomo Contarini (see G. G. ZORZI, 1965, p. 133 and 1969, pp. 64-65) resound much more meaningfully. Unequivocal evidence concerning the scientific interests of Barbaro were put forward by MAGANZA [MAGAGNÒ], ed. 1610, and by SCAMOZZI, 1583. Barbaro's relations with Palladio were earlier attested to by Gualdo. Moreover, for Barbaro's scientific approach in primis already perceived by A. DIEDO in 1817, see the comment by GARIN, 1967, p. 147.

[22] Cf. in particular, E. FORSSMAN, 1962, p. 34, and, above all, 1965, pp. 57 ff.

[23] A. PALLADIO, 1554, p. 2 r. The dogged resumption and the enlarged dimension of the survey is confirmed by GUALDO (1617, p. 9): "si diede a rivedere, misurare e considerare la bellezza e grandezza di altri edifici antichi."

[24] J. J. GLOTON, 1966, pp. 103-107.

[25] G. G. ZORZI, 1958, pp. 22-23 (cf., for an important examination, E. FORSSMAN, 1965, p. 72).

[26] M. TAFURI, 1969, pp. 126-127. Concerning the Palladian reduction (A. PALLADIO, 1570, L. II, p. 69) to a typological unity of the Vitruvian distinctions (VI, 5-6) of the suburban villa and the rustic villa, cf. E. FORSSMAN, 1965, pp. 57 ff.

[27] G. G. ZORZI, 1954, and 1969, pp. 39-50. For an examination along the lines which here concern us, cf. A. M. DALLA POZZA, 1965. BARBIERI (1970), however, has recently introduced an opportune correction, relating several drawings considered abstract to actual undertakings.

[28] We do not propose here to enter into the merits or the details of an argument that is still open, although important conclusions have been reached. Within the restricted limits of our discussion—the villas— it suffices to refer, with a choice dictated only by instrumental exigencies, to the discussion centering around Serlio by M. ROSCI (1966, pp. 33-39 and 1966 [II]), who discusses useful points of departure offered by FORSSMAN (1965, pp. 28 ff.; but cf. also the useful review by S. WILINSKI, 1969, pp. 414-423); for Cornaro, G. FIOCCO (1965, pp. 73 ff); for Falconetto, E. FORSSMAN (1966 [III]); for Giulio Romano, with wide implications, R. PALLUCCHINI (1958 and 1959). Interesting conclusions, on the level of comparison which is here implied, are drawn by B. RUPPRECHT (1963) and, above all, by M. TAFURI (1969 [II], pp. 99-109), and again by B. RUPPRECHT (1968 [II]). Cf., finally, for an overall discussion, the brilliant comments by J. S. ACKERMAN, 1966, pp. 36-80 and 1967, pp. 1-29.

[29] For a fundamental methodological indication, cf. G. C. ARGAN (1959). See, besides the comments of ACKERMAN cited in the note above (1966 and 1967), the comments of F. FRANCO

(1941, 1956, and 1959) of G. MASSON (1955), and, following the general outline of M. ROSCI (1968), of P. BIEGANSKI (1965; especially pp. 24-31, 1968, and 1969).

30 Once again, it would be out of place to develop an exhaustive discussion, since it would mean going over step by step the stages of Palladian criticism beginning with the purist censures of MILIZIA (at least 1785, pp. 64-66, whose prejudice, in spite of the efforts of CICOGNARA (1810), QUATREMÈRE DE QUINCY (1830), etc., persists, masked by the formalistic rhetoric of GUR-LITT (1914), of CANTACUZÈNE (1928), of MILANI (1928), etc. For a broader and well-reasoned collection of references see R. PANE, 1961, pp. 48-57. It is enough therefore to state that ARGAN's comments of 1930, reread in the light of the probings of 1956 and the fine notes of BETTINI (1949 and 1961 [I and II]), are resolutory and still open to rich and stimulating prospects, and to refer, for the complex discussion following from it, to the complete and well thought out review by ROSCI (1970).

31 Obviously, we do not wish here to indicate the importance of a schematic process, which is "discounted" by the oldest critical formulations of the problem of the "villa" (BANISTER FLETCHER, 1902, for example) and appears systematized in its operation in BURGER's more advanced and perceptive discusssion (1909). Burger's approach is conditioned by a decisively restrictive interpretation of the Palladian aesthetic, based upon an evolutionary principle characterized by the invention of increasingly more complex architectural types (from the *Kastelltypen* to the *Monumentelpalast*). In actuality this principle was established by Burger on the basis of a process arbitrarily divorced from factual reality, in which the type "deduced" from an overall undifferentiated examination of Palladio's works came to represent a type that determined *a priori*, and in a decisive manner, the individual aspects of Palladio's stylistic development. It is worthwhile, therefore, to emphasize, in the complete panorama, the correctness of PANE's comments (1961, pp. 223-227: Pane's position was focused and well explained in the studies of 1956, 1959, and 1964) and those of ZORZI in his monograph on the villas and theatres (1969, pp. 33-208; the formative criteria seem to me explained well in the brief note of the same year; 1969 [II], pp. 140-147, where the typological groupings serve only as instruments of exposition. In any case my preference for the quite unequivocal choice of ACKERMAN (1967, pp. 4-21 and 38-79) cannot be concealed.

32 L. PUPPI, 1966, pp. 7-12. For a recent discussion of Venetian culture during the first half of the Cinquecento, and in relation to Palladio, cf. G. FAGGIN (1967) and, for important developments, M. TAFURI (1969, pp. 128-133). It is important here to note that around the middle of the century there was a de-provincialization of the intellectual life in Vicenza, marked by lively exchanges with Venetian circles in the context of the developing awareness (which we noted in the text in regard to the Venetian circles) of the drainage of the meaning from the bourgeoisie and national-popular concepts and by the shift to cosmopolitanism (cf., in addition, P. S. LEICHT, 1933). Consequently, we are able to hypothesize a redefinition of the patronage relationship between Palladio and his Vicentine "patrons." The establishment in 1556 of the philo-Venetian Accàdemia dei Costanti, promoted by Girolamo Gualdi (a broad-minded man with a wide range of relationships at various levels, who engaged in explicit controversy with the structure of the Accademia Olimpica, which was more closed and jealous of its Vicentine identity [cf. M. MURARO, 1967, pp. 116-117]), should be considered more carefully than it has been (cf. G. PIOVENE, 1963; but J. S. ACKERMAN, 1966, pp. 31-32 takes it into account). Also, recall the exclusive attention given by WITTKOWER (1962, pp. 71 ff.) to the academicians of the Olimpia (the 1952 study by BARBIERI, pp. 257-262 is still illuminating for a profile and should be read with the register of documents by ZORZI, 1969, pp. 257-262). Think of the "pompa di sacro rito," before the Venetian Rectors, of the inauguration (G. G. ZORZI, 1969, p. 253) and the immediate echo in the Venetian area, attested by LONGIANO (1556, Dedica) and, significantly, the effect on DANIELE BARBARO (1557, Dedica), by the letter of April 3, 1557, forming the introduction to that text, by G. RUSCELLI. In works whose interest for linguistic problems (and of the rhetoric of the language) must not be undervalued, both insist on the aristocratic state of the

academicians exalted by the liberal virtue of literary *otium* ("Conti e cavalieri, quali tutti siete," however "vi gloriate più di essere chiamati Academici ... ad imitation di Marco Aurelio che a maggior lode et honore si tenne di essere chiamato filosofo che imperatore": capable of "esercitii virtuosi et nobili così nell'arme come nelle lettere"). For a complete panorama, cf. G. G. ZORZI, 1969, pp. 252-257.

33 R. WITTKOWER, 1962, pp. 74-75 and p. 73, fig. VIII. Wittkower has, moreover, refined his idea tracing the principles of Palladio's stylistic development (1961), while the hardening of a geometric interpretation can lead to the immobile abstractions of C. ROWE, 1967; M. ROSCI, 1966 (II), pp. 130-133, who opportunely refers back to FORSSMAN, 1965, pp. 57-66. Cf. also S. BETTINI, 1949, pp. 64-65. For a recapitulation on Villa Thiene, and a comparison with the Vitruvian text, cf. G. G. ZORZI, 1969, pp. 109-110.

34 S. BETTINI, 1961, p. 94.

35 Cf. in G. FIOCCO, 1965, pp. 165-167.

36 M. TAFURI, 1969, pp. 127-128; but, by the same scholar, see 1966, pp. 82-85.

37 Cf. in particular—after the obligatory reference to R. WITTKOWER, 1962, p. 74 and to W. LOTZ, 1962—B. RUPPRECHT, 1967, p. 131. The often made citation of Sangallo's palace for Lorenzo de Medici at Poggio a Caiano can lead to irrelevant conclusions (see P. HAMBERG, 1959) if it is not proposed while taking into consideration the factors that determine and differentiate the genesis of the Medici villa from Palladio's undertaking. However, we now have for the Medici villa FOSTER's accurate examination (1969) and HEYDENREICH's clarifications (1969, pp. 16-18). TAFURI's reference to Pomponazzi's "skeptical rationalism" and to his reduction of the "sacred" to "wordly value" is valid and stimulating (1969, p. 130), which takes us back to the accepted meaning of the Aristotelianism alive in Barbaro's culture.

38 A. PALLADIO, 1570, L. II, p. 69.

39 G. G. ZORZI, 1958, pp. 88-89 (and pp. 87-90, for the group of drawings of the temple); H. SPIELMANN, 1966, nn. 106 and 107 (with a reference to Trajan's Forum and a late chronology that is not shared by the author; on Palladio's relationship with the Antique cf. also POLACCO, 1965.

40 It is not here our concern to give a review of the bibliography on the Meledo villa which is, in any case, the most interesting result of the above-considered process of symbolic transference for its complex clearness, so "charged" as to be the point of departure for the breaking up and the assembly of the components (for the history of the villa, cf. G. G. ZORZI, 1969, pp. 143-147). It is useful, however, to point out the relationship established by RUPPRECHT (1968, p. 231), in the common origin, by means of Palladio's studies of the Temple of Hercules at Tivoli, to the creation of Villa Badoer. This is justified and sustained by Pane's identification (1961, p. 192) in the plan for Meledo of the landlord's house as the "conclusion" and not the "center" of the long colonnaded barns, in accordance with a purpose that is proposed again at FRATTA (cf. also M. ROSCI, 1966 [II], p. 133).

41 The Palladian texts of the Cicogna ms. are quoted, as customary, from the transcription by G. G. ZORZI, 1958, pp. 184 and 181. It is worthwhile here to note that in the rough draft of the treatise contained in the Venetian manuscript only the villas planned for Venetian nobles are recorded (G. G. ZORZI, 1958, pp. 187-188). A diffuse description of the ideology of the villa is given by RUPPRECHT, 1966; cf. also L. HEYDENREICH, 1969.

42 M. TAFURI, 1969 (II), pp. 5-6 and L. PUPPI, 1971, pp. 19-23.

43 B. ZEVI, 1963, cl. 455; cf. also S. BETTINI, 1961, and for some aspects, M. ZOCCA, 1960.

44 Cf. ZORZI's transcription, 1958, p. 185.

45 D. BARBARO, 1556, pp. 176-177.

46 G. G. ZORZI, 1965, pp. 135 and 229-230, and 1969, pp. 90-94. The information offered by the scholar on patronage (1969, p. 90) is to be carefully considered, since it seems to me to reinforce a conviction that I have had occasion to express many times in the past, especially the turn to cosmopolitanism and

the value given to aristocratic rank and the rhetorical and classicistic point of view, manifested by the organization of a numismatic collection and a private collection of worthless antiquuities, and, even more, when one thinks of the role played by the investment in land (R. GALLO, 1955, pp. 29-34, and 1956, pp. 399-400).

47 R. GALLO, 1955, p. 31, and 1956, pp. 399-400; G. G. ZORZI, 1969, p. 93.

48 G. G. ZORZI, 1969, pp. 90-91.

49 G. G. ZORZI, 1969, p. 91 (also for the quotation from the *Italia liberata dai Goti* by Trissino).

50 J. J. GLOTON, 1966, p. 107.

51 J. J. GLOTON, 1966, pp. 107-108. For a comparison with the villa by Ligorio cf. the fundamental study by D. R. COFFIN (1960); while for an attempt to recapture an indication of the stimulae that Palladio received from his probable meeting with Pirro in 1554 (see n. 24 above), cf. E. MANDOWSKY - E. MITCHELL 1963. Palladio's renewed study of Bramante's Belvedere, the ideal reconstruction of the villa, is to be regarded as of great importance, as ACKERMANN has demonstrated (1957), fully confirmed by FROMMEL (1969, pp. 47-49), and the drawings of Villa Madama, whose plan by Raphael, according to the brilliant discovery by FOSTER (1967), attests the desire to imitate the villa of the ancients (cf. D. R. COFFIN, 1967). For a recent complete review of the Roman villa, cf. FROMMEL (1969).

52 A. PALLADIO, 1570, L. II, pp. 66.

53 M. TAFURI, 1958, p. 78. The actual explicit scenographic experiences of Palladio began with the spectacles staged for the Accademia Olimpica in 1557 (G. G. ZORZI, 1969, pp. 263-264) and in 1558 (A. MAGRINI, 1847, p. 15, and G. G. ZORZI, 1969, pp. 264-265); but his theoretical interest and speculation date back much further and lead to the preparation of the illustrations for Barbaro's edition of Vitruvius (1556), after carrying out an intensive series of architectural drawings and classical restorations, as seen in RIBA X, 4 r (cf. L. PUPPI, 1963, pp. 21-28).

54 A. PALLADIO, 1570, L. II, p. 48. In fragment VI of the Cicogna ms. (in G. G. ZORZI, 1958, p. 187) the text is identical.

55 G. G. ZORZI, 1969, p. 75.

56 I believe it is useful to have a comparative table of the measurements given in the *Quattro Libri* and those in BERTOTTI SCAMOZZI (1781, plate XLI); see Appendix II.

57 Cf. G. G. ZORZI, 1961 and 1961 (II), and also R. PANE, 1961, pp. 259-276 and S. BOTTARI, 1963, pp. 28-29.

58 See the text in G. G. ZORZI, 1958, p. 181. Palladio again puts forward in the printed version of the Trattato (1570, L. II, p. 3) the same recrimination with blander words. For a note on the problem, cf. R. PANE, 1961, pp. 82-83.

59 The presence of Palladio during the construction of the loggia of the Basilica in Vicenza, the constancy of which is emphasized by the reordering of the documentary material carried out by ZORZI (1965, pp. 323-342) or the care dedicated to the Convento della Carità, which the praiseworthy work of E. BASSI has illuminated (1971), are clearly evident facts. It seems, on the other hand, that in this regard it is worthwhile to put forward again the very celebrated letter of Palladio to Vincenzo Arnaldi of February 23, 1565 (see it in A. MAGRINI, 1845, pp. 10-11 of the Appendix: doc. III)—whether it is his autograph or, as is more likely, by his son Leonida (G. G. ZORZI, 1969, p. 17, n. 100)—in which the architect sends to his correspondent a detailed "disegno ... acciò che il muraro gli intenda."

60 R. CEVESE, 1965, pp. 311-312.

61 We have not been able to find many traces of "murari" in the neighborhood of Fratta. In any case, without claiming to draw conclusions that would be improper, it should be pointed out that in the years 1562, 1563, and 1566 an "Alessandro murador" appears repeatedly in the building of the church at Fratta (APF. Libro cassa della Compagnia 1550-1582, in the file entitled *Libri 3 S. Sacramento*).

62 WITTKOWER is of a different opinion (1968, p. 345, n. 23). Accepting the supposition of Burger and of other scholars,

he affirms his suspicion that the installation is to be attributed to "post-Palladian alterations." In actuality, the raising of the loggia—the exceptionality of which has been clearly proven by PANE (1961, p. 276)—set problems at various levels which the concrete situation of the stairs resolves.

63 The escutcheon displaying the armorial bearings was replaced with the change of ownership of the villa (see Chapter III), with that of the Mocenigo family which still appears on the pediment (plate 10); the coat of arms preceding it, of which no trace has been found, was most probably destroyed.

64 The elegant solution published in 1570 obeys compositional need of an abstract design, disconnected from any reference to the site, which BERTOTTI SCAMOZZI identifies in relationship "col fine di riparare dalle inondazioni i luoghi terreni" (1781, p. 44).

65 G. LEONI, 1721, pl. XXXIII (on the edition cf. the useful comments of R. WITTKOWER, 1954); there is a balustrade at the level of the "piedestilo" on the wall joining the central block to the wings, and the profile of the tympana that closes the hemicycles is different; the statues on the arcoterion of the pediment are arranged differently.

66 J. WARE, 1738, p. XXXI; the internal stairway thus turns out to be in its right place—where it is presently and was originally—notwithstanding the fact that BERTOTTI SCAMOZZI (1781, pl. XLI: see here fig. XVII) also inexplicably places it on the right. See also n. 69 below.

67 A. MUCCI, 1791, L. II, p. 91.

68 [F. MUTTONI], 1740, pp. 21-22 and 1744, p. 29, pl. XXXII. One cannot help but observe that the author, notwithstanding the inaccuracy of the drawing in relation to the actual situation, reveals in his notations (correct indication of ownership, the navigability of the Scortico) a direct knowledge of the villa.

69 O. BERTOTTI SCAMOZZI, 1781, pp. 43-44. It is surprising, however, in the accurate drawing—next to the imprecise placement of the internal stairway (see above n. 66)—the arbitrariness of the plan of the lateral walls of the loggia, shown covered with a decoration of smooth ashlar-work which is very difficult to couple with Palladio's intention or to connect it, in examining the actual building, to a successive operation, possibly observed by Scamozzi and later obliterated.

70 O. BERTOTTI SCAMOZZI, 1781, p. 43.

71 ASV. *Giudici di Petizion* b. 379/44, n. 82 (inventory of February 17, 1675; 1676, Venetian reckoning. The guest-quarters are indicated, respectively, "vecchia" and "nuova" and consist, each one, of four "camere," although the existence of a "studiola in foresteria vecchia" is then specified. We do not derive any information from the document about whether the rooms were distributed on two floors, which cannot be excluded (for this, see n. 75).

72 T. TEMANZA, 1778, p. 362.

73 ACR. Volume marked by the letter C. *Retratti tutti del Canale Castagnaro sotto Rovigo. Indici e mappe della misurazione fatta* da D. TOMMASO FRACCARO *perito pubblico de' Possessioni de beni*, c. 61. Proportions are totally lacking in the drawing; in any case, one might recognize the front enclosing wall in the sketch, which would therefore be "separated" from the service blocks (or does that sketch portray the sequence of curbstones?).

74 ACR. Volume marked Catasto 1775. *Ritratto dello Scortico*, c. 97. The symmetrical placement of the arch and window at the conclusion of the service areas is easily attributable to a revision by the appraiser who interposes himself as well in the reproduction of the façade; nevertheless, one cannot ignore the individuation and the reproduction of the three ramps of the stairway.

75 A complex series of soundings would be necessary in order to establish not only the effective points of jointure of the extension but also of the demolitions made in order to connect the new buildings. Moreover, in a detailed examination we encounter elements that present an equal number of problems and motives for perplexity, although they do not challenge, in accordance with this author's firm conviction, the reality of the original layout and the limits of the masonry casing of the *barchesse* described in the text. For example, the great space

articulated by two pilasters in the right block might be due to an intermediate renovation when the block was split into two stories joined to the external stairway. In such an event, the jointure made between them would cause one to think that the lower space would have been adapted into a stable and the upper space into a granary or hayloft. It would then be necessary to admit that the "guest-quarters" indicated in the document cited in n. 71 would have been located in the left block on two floors and would thus explain the designation of "vecchia" (the lower floor) and "nuova" (successively organized on the upper floor, cutting vertically into the masonry block). The inventory of 1676 records, after the registration of the "foresterie" whose "camere" are further described, the existence of "granari," "caneva di vino," and "stalle" (ASV. *Giudici di Petizion* 379/44, n. 82). The question of the terracotta floor in the right wing (fig. XLVIII), similar to the floor of the hall of Palazzo Valmarana (fig. IL), should be examined; it would appear to have been autographed (M. Guiotto, 1964, p. 77).

[76] T. Temanza, 1778, p. 362.

[77] Palladio's explicit recollection (1570, L. II, p. 48) of the existence of the Castle Salinguerra could be the origin of the architect's inspiration, but in the enclosure of Villa Garzoni by Sansovino at Pontecasale we find an analogous stylization. Perhaps the present finial of the piers that mark the entrance to the garden is due to the ideas of Palladio (which does not seem quite convincing—look at the finial, much more genuine, of the piers of the back wall; but, in this event, it would settle the late decorative solution of the arcoteria of the timpana of the wings), or it could be the result of an intervention contemporary to the jointure of the extension of the wings, to which the stair between the street and the gate certainly belongs. The stair's execution is related to the raising of the street.

[78] A. F. Doni, *Attavanta*, ms., 1565 (but quoted from the 1857 edition, pp. 17 and 26-27). Cf. also A. Palladio, 1570, L. II, p. 45.

[79] G. G. Zorzi, 1958, p. 101. The drawing was earlier held

to be related to the plan of the Temple of Hercules and the correct reference to the Quadriportico of Portascura at Tivoli, called the Villa of Maecenas or of Augustus (cf. also H. Spielmann, 1966, n. 51 with a reference to the Temple of Hercules at Tivoli).

[80] L. Puppi, 1965-1966, pp 48-49.

[81] A. Palladio, 1570, L. II, p. 3.

[82] L. Puppi, 1965-1966, p. 69. For the Cornaro quotation cf. G. Fiocco, 1965, p. 156.

[83] A. Palladio, 1570, L. II, p. 3.

[84] See, for this whole question, the illuminating study by A. Chastel (1965, pp. 13-14); and cf. also 1960, where the spectacular quality of the stairway, linked to the element of surprise, is emphasized and preliminary Roman examples put forward. Cf. 1960 [II] for the individuation of clearly scenographic interests. See also C. Semenzato, 1967.

[85] Cf., along with the studies of M. Zocca (1960) and S. Bettini (1961), the perceptive comments of Tafuri (1969, pp. 130-132 and, especially, p. 135, n. 11) concerning the ideological proclamatory character of Palladio's architecture. Cf. also, for the discussion, C. Semenzato, 1967, p. 345. Cf. R. Assunto, 1963, G. Ferrara, 1968, and E. Sereni, 1962, pp. 125-128.

[86] G.C. Argan, 1956, passim. Cf. also, Zevi's extremely interesting formulation (1963, cll. 440-455, 1964), concerning which Ivanoff's inopportune interpretation is rejected (1967, p. 107).

[87] Inevitably, at this point one raises the question of Palladio and Mannerism, which in its fundamental outlines would be out of place to repropose here. See, therefore, the clear discussion by F. Barbieri (1964) and the point established by the recapitulation of Venditti (1969, pp. 42-48) and, particularly, by Rosci (1970); in the context of the broad excursus, see E. Battisti (1968-1969). The position of the author emerges in the text.

XIX - Giallo Fiorentino, *Crest of the Badoer Family*

XX - GIALLO FIORENTINO, *Crest of the Loredan Family*

XXI - GIALLO FIORENTINO, *Crest of the Loredan-Badoer alliance*

XXII - Giallo Fiorentino, *A Jester*

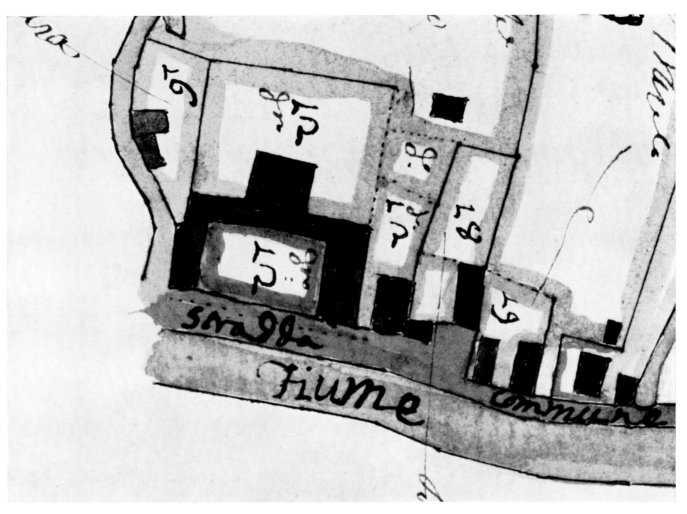

XXIII - *Plan of the complex of Villa Badoer in 1757.* From *Ritratti tutti del Canale Castagnaro...*
Historical Archives of the Commune of Rovigo, in the Concordi Library, Rovigo

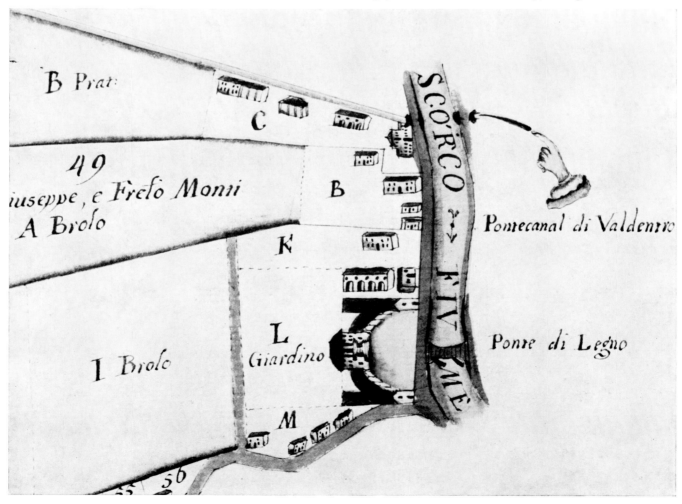

XXIV - *Bird's eye view of the complex of Villa Badoer in 1775.* From *Catasto 1775. Ritratto dello Scortico.*
Historical Archives of the Commune of Rovigo, in the Concordi Library, Rovigo

III
THE SEQUEL

The remarkable increase in the land holdings of the Badoer family was due to the sons of Francesco Badoer—whom we saw during their father's lifetime, along with Marcantonio Cornaro, personally engaged in the management of the property.[1] Such an increase, which corresponded to the growth in the economy, was a testimony of a decisive move into the area of agrarian capitalism.[2] Acquisitions of land and real estate of various types were made to increase the size of the estate at Vespara and the more recently acquired estate in Valdentro. We note a purchase on March 21, 1585, signed in Fratta "in the palace,"[3] and another on October 23, 1595, relative to a house with outbuildings.[4] Another purchase of particular importance was made on January 23, 1609. It consisted of a "landlord's house together with part of an old ruined house and another ruined building with a dovecote, and untilled farmland and garden in Fratta in the region of Castelguglielmo."[5] This was in addition to an earlier purchase of land made on June 20, 1608, in the territory of Adria.[6] Subsequent purchases were made in 1611 and 1612.[7] During the same period of time the Badoer brothers alternated, together with their associates Grimani and Cornaro, in the settlement and administration of the "reclaimed land" of the Vespara, thus providing a decisive commitment that was accepted and handed down by their heirs.[8]

In tracing the history of the family we witness the progressive transformation of the "urban" patrician. At first he retains his characteristic role in the city, while delegating to land agents and stewards the task of attending to the farm holdings which nevertheless provide the basis and economic prerequisites for that role. At this stage he permits himself only brief periods of control and longer periods of diversion and lazy pleasure. Eventually, however, he evolves into the country gentleman who personally assumes the direction of the enterprise. The seventeenth century treatise writers on agriculture, from Barpo to Agostinetti,[9] are rich in firsthand information on this subject. In equal measure the architectural theorists express the need for a different spatial organization of the villa complex. "The frequent inspection of the buildings of the estate," Scamozzi writes,[10] "is most useful to the landlords, since by means of skillful cultivation of the land one may most justly gain for oneself riches." Indeed, it is important that "at any hour the landlord may inspect his holdings, thus arousing some expectation in those who serve him that he might come at any moment. Wherefore those who manage and administer the revenues work much better and also more reliably." In response to a more complex articulation of functions, some of which were new and diverse due to the continuous presence of the landlord, the enlarged dimensions of the villa-house established, paradoxically, a relationship between the service areas and the landlord's house that tended to detach the latter and set it apart, accentuating in visual terms the distinction between duties and classes.[11]

Expressed in the previous chapter was a firm conviction that the original form of Vil-

62

CORPUS PALLADIANUM

la Badoer had not suffered serious damage for a long period of time after the construction. It was pointed out that only some changes had been made in the internal structure of the wings (scale drawing VII). It is now time to explain those changes, placing them in relation to the enlargement of the enterprise through the transfer of the services and especially the transfer of farmer and peasant lodgings to neighboring houses, which were either already there or expressly built. In short, the restoration of what were formerly the outbuildings of the villa to the needs of the landlord's residence reconfirms the late chronology of the wing extensions, which were to give the farm a new focus. But that belongs, as we will see, to a different historical phase. Annania Zen provides the information that in the middle of the 17th century the Badoers raised a prized breed of horses "in Fratta, below Rovigo."[12] But their main activity was probably the cultivation of wheat, although there must have been many opportunities to collect tolls for the bridges and other crossings that they controlled.[13] The frequency of, if not the uninterrupted residence of, the Badoers in Fratta must have been influenced by the opportunity for making decisions, not so much in the management and general supervision of the "reclaimed lands" as in the unexpected and unpredictable occasions when there were breaks and floodings of the river banks. In the early part of July of 1673 there was an especially bad "break in the banks of the Scortico in the Valdentro area." At the end of the same month Pietro di Sebastiano Badoer hurried from Fratta (where he must have lived) to Venice[14] in order to urge the Senate to help him in repairing the damage.[15] That their land holdings were the predominant interest of the family is confirmed by the fact that in the 17th century members of the family assumed political or governmental offices in that area. Among the *podestà* or mayors and captains of Rovigo and

General Directors of all of Polesine we find Andrea di Pietro Badoer in 1640 and 1641 and Sebastiano di Pietro Badoer in 1649. And we know that Andrea Badoer, after an official visit to the territory of Badia and Lendinara, feeling suddenly ill "decided to go to his most noble palace of Fratta" where shortly afterward, on April 26, 1641, he died. The condolences of the local worthies were conveyed to his brother who was "living there."[16] The selection of the Villa as a residence for lengthy periods, and also for purposes of amusement, meetings, and sumptuous receptions, is confirmed—if further proof should be necessary—by an invitation to an unnamed important personage written by Sebastiano Badoer on July 26, 1645;[17] not to mention the cordial relations maintained with illustrious families beyond the Po, such as the Bentivoglio.[18] The male line of the Badoer family became extinct on October 2, 1678, with the death of Giuseppe Gaetano, then still a child.[19] His father Pietro had died three years earlier,[20] and on February 7, 1676, on the petition of his widow, Cecilia Giustiniani, a judicial inventory of the real property of the estate was drawn up for the protection of the female heirs. The document can be utilized to establish that the original form of the villa at that date must not have suffered damage. We can add that the presence of cumbersome furniture and pictures on the walls of the rooms of the main building lead us to believe that the fresco decorations, which we will discuss in Part II, had already been covered over.[21] In any case, the distribution of the rooms beginning with the "loggia above the great stair" is intact both on the *piano nobile* (the "great hall," the "large rooms," the "rooms," and the "small rooms") and on the lower floor (the "servants' dining room," the "storeroom," the "kitchen," the "laundry room"). Moreover, we learn that the entrance door was glazed and that "in the gardens" in front and in back of the villa there were numerous "pots... with lemon and orange trees placed on marble pedestals." Other pots with plants of "jasmine and myrtle and carnations" were placed "on the walls of the fishpond," the location of which, whether in the garden in front or behind, is not specified. By this time the two fountains, one crowned by a nude male figure (Neptune, plate 42) and the other by a nude female figure (Amphitrite?, plate 43), must already have been in place. The fountains are of modest workmanship and, on the basis of style and taste, datable, with caution, in the first half of the Seicento.[22]

Following the death of little Giuseppe Gaetano Badoer the appraisal and division of the property among the Badoer sisters took place between June 10 and September 28, 1681. This was done in order to allot a dowry to Lucrezia di Pietro on the occasion of her marriage to Alvise di Giorgio Priuli. The share comprising "the palace located in the land of Fratta, with guest quarter, lodgings of the land agents or stewards, with gardens, cultivated fields, warehouses, granaries, stables, carriage houses and other effects..." went to Paolina, the wife of Marcantonio Mocenigo, into whose family the villa then passed.[23] The villa, as stated before, did not suffer damage. The plan by Bertotti Scamozzi, which we have so often cited, shows that it remained intact in its layout (figs. XV-XVII).[24] Within the limits of the use that the new proprietors had to make of it, the functions did not change. In substance the assemblage of the tasks organized and supervised by earlier owners remained the same, although there was a tendency to exalt the villa's role as a place of repose, diversion, and country holidays—the hospitality extended to Eugene of Savoy being significant in this respect.[25] And, in relation to its predominant use for entertainment, they had the ceilings of the *piano nobile* lowered with "vaults that had

only one foot of decoration."[26] Research concerning the transfer of the edifice from the Mocenigo family to others (in all probability the Delvecchio family who were in possession of the villa at the beginning of the 19th century, has not been pursued to the point of determining the time and manner in which it came about.[27] Probably the new change in ownership is attributable to the catastrophic events in the history of Venice that brought about a rapid decline in the presence of the Venetian aristocracy on the mainland and the liquidation of their landed properties.[28] The drastic modification of the wings of the villa (fig. XXXI) occurred, as far as we can tell, after 1775-1780 (figs. XXIII-XXIV; scale drawing XIIIb). These alterations can be attributed to the successors of the Mocenigo family and to the objective needs for a new type of operation, postulating the supervision of the family that possessed the villa and an administrative establishment of reduced dimensions whose productivity is aimed at economic self-sufficiency. Thus, it demanded a concentration of service that would nevertheless, in re-articulating the space to the functions, have been guided by the need to obey the rules of decorum. No information has been found that would establish an exact chronology of those events which very probably took place at the end of the century, nor has the identity of the architect been discovered. But during that crucial period a certain Bellettato[29] often worked in Fratta, and there between 1783 and 1784 we meet the much more suggestive name of Sante Baseggio.[30] The problem, although certainly not irrelevant, is of a level that will permit an approximate answer. In regard to the buildings that form the extensions of the wings, in formal terms they are guided by a desire for an evocative adaptation of the Palladian design. But in achieving this adaptation a neoclassic vocabulary charged with elements from late

Mannerism was used. It is enough to note in these additions the definitions of the areas designated for the stalls and the chapel (figs. XXVI-XXVII)[31] and to point out that, in the course of time and in answer to the changes of ownership and administration, subsequent modifications had to be brought about in the general design of the central block of the villa—a design which had already been compromised. Meanwhile, the raising of the street level negated, and continues to negate, the original scenographic manner in which the villa dominated the site (fig. XXV). Now, however, thanks to the meritorious restoration undertaken by the *Ente per le Ville Venete* the *piano nobile* has been brought back to its original state.[32]

NOTES TO CHAPTER III

[1] ACL. *Archivio Vecchio di Vespara*. On February 4, 1563 (1564 - Venetian reckoning) "miser Marco Antonio Badoero," with Marcantonio Cornaro and Francesco Grimani, appears as a "consorte" of the Vespara in a document of the Provveditori sopra Beni Inculti, which issues an order to "Iseppo dei Pontoni e Francesco di Treviggi ingegneri" to make a sketch of the areas destined to benefit from a "pontecanal e uno scolador" (cf. the document in B. RIGOBELLO, *Origini del Retratto*, ms., p. 2). We have not been able to trace, at the place where it should be, the topographical drawing (ASV. *Provveditori sopra Beni Inculti: Disegni. Padova e Polesine*, passim). For the presence of Marcantonio cf. the above-cited study by Rigobello; but also, BCV. Mss. PD c. 2346/VII, in file containing documents relative to the bitter dispute that arose about the carrying into effect of the "sotto ponte canale sotto il fiume del Scortego" which was resolved July 15, 1572. (There are some drawings, but they are irrelevant to our purposes.)

[2] Cf., in particular, S. J. WOOLF, 1962, especially p. 437.

[3] ASV. *Privati: Badoer*. Volume marked I, a document of September 28, 1681, by the notary Antonio Petrazzolo.

[4] ASV. *Privati: Badoer*. Volume marked *Cattastico Badoer*: c. 9, of that date, from the register of a deed by the notary Marin Filippi di Rovigo.

[5] *Ibid., idem*: c. 9, of that date, from the register of a deed by the notary Beazoni di Venezia.

[6] BCV. Mss. PD c. 2617/VII: of that date, from the original parchment.

[7] ASV. *Privati: Badoer*. Volume marked *Cattastico Badoer*: c. 9, of November 9, 1611 (Palladio buys a small piece of cultivable land), May 1612 (Palladio buys another plot), August 28, 1612 (Palladio buys real estate and land in Bragola). Drawn from the register of deeds of the notaries Cesare Vega and Filippo Filippi of Rovigo. The income of the Polesane estates was partly committed by the Badoers, initially, to investments in leaseholds, as is indicated by the will of Giovanni dictated September 30, 1609 (ASV. *Notarile: Testamenti. Fabrizio Benazzano* b. 57, n. 318). Cf., for the necessary correction, L. PUPPI, 1965-1966, p. 62.

[8] See, for the complete *dossier* on the question, B. RIGOBELLO, *Origini del Retratto*, ms., passim. The material is from the Archivio Vecchio of Vespara at the ACL. Other documentation is in the BCV. Mss. PD 2346/VII (see in particular the file entitled *1642 Copie di conti esistenti nel libro di Zuane Badoer cassiere del Retratto Vespara e Presciana del 1637 sin 1642*, etc.). Further confirmation is in the land tax declaration shown by Pietro q. Sebastiano Badoer and Lucrezia Mocenigo relicta q. Sebastiano (ASV. *X Savi alle Decime: Redecima* 1661 b. 214, Condizione n. 1058). The holdings in Polesine are shown to be enormously increased and "Valdentro nel ritratto di Lendinara nelle Valli di S. Biasio" is mentioned, among others.

[9] G. B. BARPO, 1634, passim, but particularly pp. 25-27; G. AGOSTINETTI, 1681, passim.

[10] V. SCAMOZZI, 1615, p. I, L. III, pp. 266-285.

[11] Cf. the careful analysis of A. VENTURA, 1969, pp. 69 ff.

[12] A. ZEN, 1658, p. 11.

[13] For example, a document of November 9, 1644 (kindly pointed out by A. Bellettato, whose location I do not know), mentions the sale at auction by the commune of Fratta to the Badoers of the "ponte e pesso della Fratta sopra il fiumicello detto Scortico," the rights to which were given up by Francesco Badoer on January 27, 1660 (1661 Venetian reckoning). (ASV. *Privati: Badoer*. Volume marked *Cattastico Badoer*: c. 43, at the date.) In 1681, however, listed in the name of the Badoer heirs are numerous "livelli che si scode lungo il canaletto Scortico" (*ibid., idem*. Volume marked I, in file entitled *1681, 28 settembre*).

[14] APF. *Registro Atti Battesimo 26 ottobre 1665 - 21 gennaio 1677*: drawn from a "memoria" inserted between the pages of the volume. In the cited land tax declaration of 1661, Pietro Badoer names "la casa dominicale in Villa della Fratta con sue habentie e pertinenze serve per uso" (ASV. *X Savi alle Decime: Redecima* 1661 b. 214, Condizione n. 1058).

[15] C. SILVESTRI, *Storia agraria*, ms., vol. III, p. 313. In the "decreto dell'eccellentissimo Senato 11 luglio 1673 fu deliberator ch'egli a sue spese otturasse la rotta, premendogli a maggior segno di liberar il suo palazzo nella Fratta...." Naturally Badoer arranges to obtain compensation for the estimated expense, by means of the tax on salt, payed by the commune of Fratta.

[16] G. DURAZZO, 1865, pp. 29-30. A commemorative tablet was dedicated to Sebastiano "sopra il campanile di piazza" in Rovigo, dated 1651, and quoted by CAMPANELLA (*Delle iscrizioni pubbliche e private*, ms., c. 7, n. XXXI). For the account of the death of Palladio, see ACR. *Registro Atti del Consiglio*, marked M, at the date.

[17] BCR. Fondo Concord, pp. 324-364, at the name (n. 16). The text read: "Secondo li comandi di Vostra Signoria Illustrissima l'invio il meso per aviso che la caroza sarà al castello di qua dal passo, atendendola dimani per ricever suoi commandi. Sempre me li confermo servire, di Vostra Signoria Illustrissima divotissimo servitor Sebastian Badoer. Frata li 26 luglio 1645."

The document comes from the Bentivoglio Archives in Ferrara, so possibly the addressee was a member of that family.

[18] BCR. Fondo Concord, pp. 324-364, at the name (n. 15). Drawn from a note sent by Pietro Badoer November 28, 1668, from Venice to Marquis Ippolito Bentivoglio recommending to him "Pré Girolamo Legname de' Minimi" who was going on a trip to Ferrara.

[19] ASV. *Privati: Badoer*. Volume marked I, in a loose sheet marked Genealogia Badoer. The boy was born, after the death of the father, on November 2, 1675.

[20] *Ibid., idem.*

[21] We do not have, obviously, any precise information: ASV. *Giudici di Petizion* b. 379/44, n. 82. In any event, BERTOTTI SCAMOZZI (1781, p. 44) makes a precise reference to an "intonacatura a bianco," which, however, could relate to the lowering of the ceilings (see below n. 26).

[22] ASV. *Giudici di Petizion* b. 379/44, n. 82. We learn among other things that in the "loggia" were "banchi dipinti" n. 8 and that the entrance door to the hall was glazed ("una tortiera con cristalli nuova per la porta del palazzo," in place of the "portiera vecchia rotta con vetri serviva per la suddetta porta"), etc. Any attribution for the statues would be, in our present state of knowledge, premature. We can say only that they do not appear to be extraneous to the iconographic program of the frescoes in the villa where representations and "istorie" of marine gods (and especially gods of the forest and lake) appear. See, for an allegorical connection of Neptune to the general idea of water (sea, fountain, river, and lake), RIPA, 1618, p. 102.

[23] ASV. *Privati: Badoer*. Volume marked I, in file entitled *1681, 28 settembre* (the text refers to a "dissegno" of the assessors, that is unfortunately lost). The complexity of the Fratta enterprise appears from the description of other portions of the estate in which services certainly appertaining to the complex gravitating around the villa are included; for example, "la casa in la Fratta dove soleva abittar li fattori," etc. We note in passing that Cecilia Giustinian Badoer has legal work done in Fratta, including the drawing up of deeds of purchase (for example, ASV. *Privati: Badoer*. Volume marked *Cattastico Badoer*, c. 9, on June 10, 1683) until shortly before 1687, at which date she was dead.

[24] O. BERTOTTI SCAMOZZI, 1781, pp. 43-45.

[25] [F. MUTTONI], 1740, p. 22. Cf. for the importance of the thus vouched for relationship, H. TIETZE, 1933.

[26] O. BERTOTTI SCAMOZZI, 1781, p. 44. The ceiling, the author emphasizes, "sarebbero coper[ti] con le impalcature di legno" (trusting in PALLADIO, 1570, L. II, p. 48, who calls them "di solaro," which the recent restoration shows they are) if it were not for the unfortunate lowering, which must have been part of a larger operation, presumably undertaken for reasons of comfort (heating, etc.). In fact, BERTOTTI SCAMOZZI (*ibid.*) provides the information that "sopra di questo piano [nobile] vi sono comodi appartamenti di stanzini, che il Palladio aveva destinati per granai, e che presentemer :e sono impiegati a più conveniente et utile uso." That serves as proof of the intervention during the Mocenigo proprietorship, since the inventory of 1676 says nothing about upper "stanzini." To this same interior modification belongs the arrangement, over the door to the principal room, of the four busts supported by a corbel, recorded by BELLETTATO (*Villa Badoer*, ms., p. VII) and now lost, which represented the Seasons. They would have been of the 18th century.

[27] A. MAGRINI, 1845, p. LXXII.

[28] M. BERENGO, 1955, pp. 88-130 and passim.

[29] Several documents in the APF tell us, on the basis of concrete evidence, of the activities of this person who was adept in his profession and culturally in tune with his times.

[30] APF. Book marked A. of the *Capitoli*, in Cartella P, 1783-1787, cc. 94-95, at the date of March 12, 1782, and *Memorie* 1761-1787, at the date of December 25, 1784, and of April 3, 1785. Cf., on the architect, the fine thesis of G. FOLCO PIZZO (*Sante Baseggio*, ms.; and on his presence in Fratta, pp. 49-63).

[31] The chapel was placed in the front section of the south *barchessa* (cf. also A. C. BELLETTATO, *Villa Badoer*, ms., p. VII). It is worthwhile to point out in order to state again the late chronology of the extensions, that the Badoers possessed a "giesiola" (chalk-pit) near to the "Bragolla" holdings, which passes, through Paolina, to the Mocenigo family. (ASV. *Privati: Badoer*. Volume marked I, in file entitled *1681, 28 settembre*.)

[32] Concerning the acquisition of the villa by the Ente per le Ville Venete, cf. G. MAZZOTTI, 1962, p. 824, and concerning the restorations, M. GUIOTTO, 1964, pp. 76-78.

Part II

I

GIALLO FIORENTINO THE PAINTER
NOT JACOPO DEL GIALLO
THE ILLUMINATOR

Palladio explicitly states that the rooms of the villa "have been decorated... by Giallo Fiorentino."[1] The need to pinpoint this person, to narrow down the genericism of Palladio's reference, has been faced by scholars who, starting from the entry in Thieme-Becker, have almost unanimously decided that he is to be identified with the manuscript illuminator Jacopo del Giallo. Before entering into the merits of the iconographic and stylistic facts represented by the decoration itself, which the recent restoration has brought to light, it is advisable to look again from all angles at this question of authorship. This can lead, on the basis of an analysis of the data available, to a new and unexpected solution.

Our knowledge of Jacopo del Giallo the manuscript illuminator is the result of a rather historiographical and critical development. He was introduced by Milanesi in a fragmentary autobiography of Raffaello da Montelupo which Milanesi republished as a clarification and an enrichment of Vasari's Life of Palladio.[2] In his autobiography Raffaello da Montelupo recalls the trip that he made as a young man from Florence to Rome with Giovanni del Trombetta and Jacopo d'Antonio Giallo. Milanesi was able to ascertain through his research that the name of "Jacopo Giallo son of Antonio di Jacopo Giallo" was registered in the *Libro Rosso dei debitori e creditori* of Florence in 1520 and in the *Vecchio Libro dell'Arte* in 1523.[3] He was also able to give a stylistic existence to this figure, thanks to the recovery of several works which permitted him to assign Jacopo's activity to the field of manuscript illumination. These works include a missal, now in the Casanatense Library in Rome, which was illuminated for Cardinal Francesco Cornaro between 1538 and 1539, and which contains, on *carta* 133 in the decoration of the letter "C" of the word *Cibavit*, the signature "Ia.º Ga.º."[4] There is also a choir book, formerly in S. Giorgio Maggiore in Venice, which is signed on the first page (now stolen, but attested to by Cicogna) with the inscription "Jaco Grillo f. 1538."[5] Furthermore, there is the *Commissione Giovanni da Lezze* in the Correr Library in Venice.[6] These examples, for the most part, solidly link the Florentine illuminator to the Venetian area. After Bradley's rather unimportant contribution,[7] the attempt to provide an improved outline based on new information is due to Hadeln.[8] He accepted the Florentine origin of the artist and his presence in Venice between 1520 and 1525, and provided an enriched confirmation of Milanesi's account by the recovery of the record of final payment for the *Commissione da Lezze* of April 21, 1539.[9] The German scholar then verified the registration of the master in the records of the Venetian *Fraglia* or Painters' Guild, correcting with happy insight the erroneous transcription of Moschini (*Giacomo del Fallo*) in the text he had to reckon with[10] which is without an exact date but which, from the evidence, was done after 1530. Hadeln also tracked down further documentation of the illuminator's presence in Venice on June 16 and December 24 of 1538 and, apparently, on January 31, 1554 (1555—Venetian reckoning) when the fiscal authorities recorded the name of a *Giallo depentore fiorentino*.[11] Moreover, Hadeln established, on the basis of the writings of Nicolò Franco and Aretino, the high degree of esteem that the illuminator enjoyed among the intellectual circles of Venice that were interested in artistic questions. The facts are of great interest. Franco writes in August 1539 in *Dialogo VIII*: "If you become a painter, and do not come up to Titian you will not be the first in your field. If you are an architect and do not become a Serlio, you will not be commended for the perfection of your works... And if as an illuminator you are not the equal of Giallo you will be neither unique or singular."[12] Even more significant are the words of Pietro Aretino—significant because they are pronounced within the context of a close friendship with the artist. On May 23, 1537 in Venice, addressing Jacopo as "Dear Brother," Aretino recalls the manuscript illuminations executed by Jacopo for a *Book of Offices* "with gold covers [by Cellini] made for Card. Ippolito dei Medici of glorious memory, and given by Pope Paul [III] to His Majesty [Charles V] when he was in Rome," and another set of manuscript illuminations done for Aretino himself on a copy of the *Stanze* and made in honor of Isabelle of Austria—a volume which the writer intended to give to the sovereign.[13] "I am not blind in regard to painting; many times Raphael and Fra Bastiano and Titian have followed my judgment ... and I know that the illuminators follow the designs of the masters of stained glass and their way of working is no more than [the creation] of decorations made of ultramarine and green blue, of cochineal lacquers and ground gold, and of working them into an embellishment, frieze or scroll, and similar simple little things. But your work is all design and all relief. Everything in it is sweet, delicately shaded, as if done in oils."[14] And on June 7, 1542, rejoicing in the birth of the artist's son, he declares he is sure that "such a baby will inherit that excellent talent of illuminating, which, in the design, the diligence, the delicacy and the honored and marvelous style of the works that continuously come from your hand, amaze and astonish the most expert judges and the most acute eyes."[15] The citations are purposely reproduced at length since from the complete comments we obtain a portrait of the master as an illuminator and only as an illuminator, with statements so emphatic that they leave no margin for diverse inclinations and operations in the field of painting, which would certainly have been reported. Probably on the basis of such considerations, Hadeln—who does not seem to have grasped the significance of the professional designation of *depentore* in the 1555 document—continues to reiterate his own doubts about a possible identification of Jacopo del Giallo the illuminator with Giallo Fiorentino the decorator who, according to Palladio, was at Fratta.[16] However, Levi D'Ancona has discounted these doubts.[17] This position was followed unanimously by the specialists—the present author included[18]—with the exception of Crosato.[19] Jacopo's personality thus grows quantitatively to the detriment of its quality and coherence. He immediately assumes the polymorphic physiognomy of an artist with the ability to move with ease between diverse techniques. If during the years of 1534-1535 and 1539 one restores to him a period of activity in Rome in the modest undemanding role of a painter of pennants and draperies[20] (earlier than and concomitant with his presence in the Venetian area where his specialty would be as an illuminator recognized not only by the prestigious intellectuals but also by the State which appointed him to an official position), the change to the extremely different technique of fresco painting exercised in a late phase of his career is still not exceptional. To

XXV - *Villa Badoer: Over-all view*

XXVI - *Villa Badoer: View of the left wing*

XXVII - *Villa Badoer: View of the right wing*

XXVIII - *Villa Badoer: Capital and entablature of the Tuscan Order in the colonnade*

XXIX - *Villa Badoer: Base of a column of the Tuscan Order in the colonnade*

XXX - *Villa Badoer: Detail of the right colonnade*

XXXI - *Villa Badoer: View of the area in front of the main block, with the right wing in the background.*

XXII - *Villa Badoer: Outbuildings and colonnade of the right wing, seen from above*

XXXIII - *Villa Badoer: Rear view of the right wing*

XXXIV - *Villa Badoer: Outbuildings and colonnade of the left wing, seen from above*

XXXV - *Villa Badoer: Detail of a baluster*
of the main stairway leading up to the villa

XXXVI - *Villa Badoer: Detail of a balustrade*
of the main starway

XXXVII - *Villa Badoer: Aedicule*
in the enclosing wall at the rear

XXXVIII - *Villa Badoer: Aedicule*
in the enclosing wall at the rear

XXXIX - Villa Badoer: Left wing
showing point of juncture
of various elements, seen from the rear

XL - Villa Badoer: Right wing,
showing point of juncture of various
elements, seen from the rear

XLI - *Villa Badoer: A service room on the ground floor*

XLII - *Villa Badoer: The kitchen on the ground floor*

XLIII - *Villa Badoer: A corridor on the ground floor*

XLIV - *Villa Badoer: The kitchen on the ground floor*

XLV - *Villa Badoer: Articulation of space on the ground floor*

XLVI - *Villa Badoer: The service room illustrated in fig. XLI, seen from the opposite point of view*

XLVII - *Villa Badoer: The stairway leading from the ground floor to the main floor*

XLVIII - *Villa Badoer: Detail of the pavement in the right wing*

IL - *Vicenza, Palazzo Valmarana Braga: Detail of the pavement of the Great Hall on the main floor*

L - *Villa Badoer: A well head*

prove it there is an indispensable moment in his career surpassing even the Fratta commission. Thus we end by reducing and absorbing into the personality praised by Franco and Aretino, the personality of the "Painter named dal Zallo" who, according to Ridolfi,[21] collaborated with Giuseppe Salviati in the decoration of the façade of Palazzo Loredan at S. Stefano.[22] One must say nevertheless that Levi D'Ancona was still able to attribute the *Commissione di Girolamo Venier* (dated March 1555 and now at the Marciana Library) to Jacopo,[23] not permitting the "late" option for the fresco technique to appear to be a definitive one which would render it suspect—an improbable, abrupt change of course. Actually we must recognize with Shakespeare that "there are more things in heaven and earth than are dreamt of in our philosophy."

Reason for doubt would not have been lacking if the facts had been considered more carefully, and that applies also and especially to the present writer. It suffices, in looking again at one of these ill-considered facts, to recall the care with which the sources, both archival and literary, allude to the matter of professional status. The designation of *miniador* (illuminator) or *depintore* (painter) is never casual; it refers to the rights of an order still profoundly, although distantly, influenced by the traditions of a corporative work organization.[24] In this case we must agree that it is highly improbable that one may be able to equate the *Zallo depentore* we encounter in 1555 with the *Jacomo del Zalo* (or *del Giallo* or *dal Zallo*) *miniador* who enrolled in the *Fraglia* or Corporation, was recorded in documents of 1538 and 1539, was exalted by Franco in 1539 and praised by Aretino in 1537 and 1542. But by good fortune there is evidence that resolves the question —evidence that, incredible as it sounds, has been ignored until now by everyone, in spite of the correct emphasis given to it by

the editors of Aretino's correspondence. Jacopo del Giallo *miniador* was already dead in 1545. Pietro Aretino's own words tell us so unequivocally. In November of 1545, writing to Antonio Bernieri, a pupil of Giallo, Pietro exhorts his correspondent, who was ill, to take care of himself, "since if you were not here, the world would feel—as it now does not feel—the loss of Giallo messer Jacopo, your preceptor. 'Now does not feel,' I say, because you have taken his place, and being in art, of such lofty diligence, patience and intelligence as he was earlier, it does not seem to us that he ever died."[25] Returning Jacopo to the ranks of illuminators by an opportune revision, we are left with "Zallo depentore fiorentin" who in 1555 "lives in the district of S. Moritio" in "a house" he rented from Leonardo Bollani for "11 ducats" a year.[26] He is the one who finally, without forcing the matter, must be recognized as the fresco painter of Fratta and Salviati's "companion." Patient, consistent archival research has not up to now led to documentary information to sustain or further embellish the three meager points of reference available to us.[27] In order to place Giallo "the Painter" within the coordinates of the Venetian cultural world around the middle of the Cinquecento, there is only one certain work to fall back on—and we will do so in the next chapter—after having risked some hypotheses which need to be verified on the basis of concrete facts. Crosato wondered if the master was not by chance the brother of the illuminator, and the question is not only sensible but subtle.[28] There is the coincidence of the last name, or nickname, which leads one to think of a common origin in Florence. Also, and here we anticipate ourselves, there is a participation in the same stylistic background and tastes which would have surely facilitated in due course the reduction to a common denominator of the secure works by the illuminator (starting from the *Commissione da Lezze* in the Correr, etc.) and of the decorations at Fratta. In Giallo the painter we could imagine recognizing a possible son of Jacopo the illustrator, though not the son born in 1542 who would have been too young to collaborate with Salviati and to paint the frescoes for Palladio's villa. A tie of kinship, whatever it might be, can be conceded on the basis of the considerations we have presented, but there is still another important reason. Jacopo del Giallo moved within a circle of patronage that implied the presence of members of the same aristocratic families which would later, as far as one can ascertain, involve Giallo the Painter. We recall Jacopo's work for Cardinal Francesco Cornaro, who was related through his sister's marriage to the Loredan family, and the work he did for Giovanni da Lezze, who was also associated with the Loredans.[29] Also, the friendship and approval of a Franco and an Aretino must be read as a mark of the "Grand Manner." Further along in time Giallo's activity falls, more specifically, within the context of the cosmopolitan cultural ambience. For the purpose of a non-generic identification it is sufficient to recall the role played by the Grimani family[30]—close relations of both the Badoers and the Loredans—who were eventually involved with Giuseppe Salviati and Giallo. Although it has not been possible to refer to a specific individual responsibility for the summons which brought the two masters together to fresco the outside walls of Palazzo Loredan at S. Stefano (nor has it been possible to pinpoint the chronology of the undertaking), here, thanks to Ridolfi's convincing information,[31] we can

grasp an important problem. The Loredans acquired the edifice after 1539,[32] the year when the Tuscan artist came to Venice.[33] During the period when Badoer's project at Fratta was under way, Giuseppe Salviati was caught up in the "circle" of Daniele Barbaro and had established contact with Palladio. Salviati was being called on by the families of the aristocracy at the same time that they came to Palladio to ask him to provide an architectural expression for their way of life. In 1552 Salviati dedicated to Patriarch Elect Barbaro his own small book on "Instructions on how to make a perfect volute with a compass."[34] In return he received praise which took on, in the final analysis, the sense of public recognition of citizenship in the demanding circle of the classicists. It also secured for him an invitation to participate, along with Palladio, in the 1556 edition of Vitruvius.[35] With scarcely veiled words Barbaro, in Palladio's name, did not hesitate to confirm his appreciation for Salviati's commitment to the correct definition of forms and to praise him "for the marvelous effects of the centers of the volute."[36] The same Palladio had friendly relations with Giacomo Contarini who had welcomed in his house in S. Samuele the "most excellent Iseppe Salviati."[37] We see then, in conclusion, that in order to finish with a suitable decorative program the "noble palace" at Fratta, the architect turned to the circle around Salviati who was trustworthy, well known, and appreciated by the patrons. He did this by calling on Giallo the Painter, who was not relegated to a subordinate place in the studio, but who appears to have enjoyed a position of credit and prestige.

NOTES TO CHAPTER I

¹ A. PALLADIO, 1570, L. II, p. 48.

² G. MILANESI, 1906, vol. IV, p. 557.

³ G. MILANESI, 1906, vol. IV, p. 557, n. 4 (the first edition of Milanesi's massive work is of 1879).

⁴ G. MILANESI, 1906, vol. IV, p. 558, n.

⁵ G. MILANESI, 1906. vol. IV, p. 558, n. For the reference see E. A. CICOGNA, 1824-1853, vol. IV, p. 376. However, Milanesi reports incorrectly the text of the signature that Cicogna published by changing, without further ado, "Grillo" into "Giallo." BRADLEY (1888, p. 68), on the other hand, adheres strictly to the reading "Grillo," not taking into consideration the possibility of an error on Cicogna's part and produces a miniature painter with the name Jacopo Grillo influencing LEVI D'ANCONA (1962, [II], p. 161), who at first accepts and accredits the double designation "Jacopo d'Antonio Giallo o Grillo."

⁶ G. MILANESI, 1906, vol. IV, p. 558, n. The scholar then enriches the catalogue of the illuminator with the reasonable attributions (ibid.) of the "Commissione a Giovanni Antonio Tagliapietra" of 1539 and "di Giovanni Cappello," of 1540, both at the Correr.

⁷ J. W. BRADLEY, 1888, p. 68 (and see n. 5 above).

⁸ D. v. HADELN, 1911, pp. 166-167.

⁹ D. v. HADELN, 1911, pp. 166-167, where the text is reported correctly; "Maistro Jacomo dal Zalo miniador," for 16 ducats (ASV. Procuratia de Supra: Cassier Chiesa reg. 2, on the date cf. also M. LEVI D'ANCONA, 1962 [II], p. 162).

¹⁰ D. v. HADELN, 1911, p. 166. For Moschini's text see in BCV. Mss. Moschini XIX, c. 4 r. It is a matter of copies taken in 1815 from the "libri della Veneta Accademia," published in a confused and partial manner by NICOLETTI (1890) and republished in a complete and precise manner by PIGNATTI (1965).

¹¹ D. v. HADELN, 1911, pp. 166-167.

¹² N. FRANCO, 1590, pp. 111 r - v. The theme of the dialogue is "insegnare con ogni facilità tutte le arti, tutte le scienze, e il vero modo di ascendere a tutti i gradi."

¹³ P. ARETINO, 1597-1960, vol. I, pp. 45-46. The accurate clarifications are by the editors P. PERTILE and E. CAMESACA.

¹⁴ Ibid.

¹⁵ P. ARETINO, 1957-1960, vol. I, pp. 212-213.

¹⁶ D. v. HADELN, 1911, p. 167. The scholar is even more dubious in the commentary (1914-1924, vol. I, p. 241, n. 6) to RIDOLFI, 1648, p. 242, n.

¹⁷ M. LEVI D'ANCONA, 1962.

¹⁸ L. PUPPI, 1965-1966, pp. 54-56. Also ZORZI (1969, pp. 97-98) confirms the identification.

¹⁹ L. CROSATO, 1962, p. 51.

²⁰ M. LEVI D'ANCONA, 1962, p. 1.

²¹ C. RIDOLFI, 1648, vol. I, pp. 241-242.

²² M. LEVI D'ANCONA, 1962, p. 18; L. PUPPI, 1965-1966, pp. 54-55.

²³ M. LEVI D'ANCONA, 1962, p. 15.

²⁴ The official entry of the illuminators in the painters' guild comes about in 1574, when on March 14 one of their members appears in the "banca" (ASV. Arti: Dipintori b. 103 [Mariegola], cc. 58 r and v; BCV. Mss. IV, 163, c. 46 r). Obviously, from that date a process of symbiosis begins, which will liquidate the strict distinctions in the professional qualifications which

earlier prevailed. Cf., among others, D. BROTTI, 1901, p. 82 and A. NIERO, 1965.

²⁵ P. ARETINO, 1957-1960, vol. II, pp. 120-121. Cf. the emphasis of BERTILE-CAMESASCA, 1957-1960, vol. III, t. 2, pp. 336-337. Unfortunately, the exact date of Jacopo's death is not ascertainable from the Venetian death records of the Provveditori alla Sanità which for the years 1539-1550 is full of gaps (ASV. Sanità: Necrologi reg. 794-795). On Bernieri cf. the meager, unsigned entry in THIEME BECKER, 1909.

²⁶ D. v. HADELN, 1911, p. 167. See the fiscal account in ASV. X Savi alle Decime: Redecima 1537 b. 122, Condizione aggiunta ordinaria n. 2582.

²⁷ The declaration of Leonardo Bollani to the fiscal authorities presented in February 1557 (1538 - Venetian reckoning) and February 15, 1540 (1541 - Venetian reckoning), state "in San Moricio do casette," rented first for five ducats a piece and then for four (ASV. X Savi alle Decime: Redecima 1537 reg. 364, n. 275 and n. 199). Evidently they were deteriorating in such a rapid and serious way as to make a complete restoration advisable. This was in fact done before 1555, when the two small buildings were reduced to just one, revaluated, and put up for rent for eleven ducats. For our purposes this episode yields very little, except that Giallo was living in Bollani's house after 1541. Our ignorance of his given name and the Christian name of his father constitutes an insurmountable obstacle in tracing him down among the artists recorded in the guild.

²⁸ L. CROSATO, 1962, p. 51.

²⁹ See chap. 1, n. 30.

³⁰ See chap. 1, n. 31. Cf. V. MARPILLERO, 1937; W. REARICK, 1959, passim, and in the fundamental synthesis of R. PALLUCHINI, 1950, passim. Very useful, and characteristic, is the study by SCHULZ, 1961.

³¹ The absence of Zallo's name from Sansovino's "guidebook" (1581, p. 143 v) and from the editions amplified by STRINGA (1604, p. 262 v) and MARTINIONI (1663, p. 386), which mention only Salviati, does not weaken in my opinion the credibility we must accord to Ridolfi; if anything, by proving the greater abundance of his information, it enhances his credibility.

³² G. LORENZETTI, 1956, p. 497: Lorenzetti does not cite the sources for his statement which, in any case, are not given by the nineteenth century historians. Cf., for example, G. I. FONTANA, 1865, pp. 403-404. The same FONTANA (1967 ed., p. 256) erroneously, in consequence of evident confusion, states the presence of Sante Zago in the decoration of Palazzo Loredan; the quid pro quo is taken up, without discussion, by L. FOSCARI, 1936, pp. 88-90.

³³ For useful information on Salviati's arrival in Venice, see the fine studies of CHENEY (1963, passim) and of M. HIRST (1963, passim).

³⁴ G. PORTA, 1552 Dedica.

³⁵ D. BARBARO, 1556, unnumbered pages at the end. Cf. the notes of ZORZI (1958, p. 126; and also, 1965, p. 99) and, to enlarge and clarify the sphere of Salviati's cultural relationships (to Marcolini, for example), A. BALLARIN, 1967, p. 86. Also recall the document brought forward by GONZATI (1852, vol. I, p. 61, doc. XLIII); it consists of a letter by "Iseppo" to Marco Mantova Benavides of November 27, 1573, in which indications of friendly relationships with Girolamo Campagna and Danese Cattaneo appear.

36 D. BARBARO, 1556, *ibid*. The Patriarch Elect writes: "Havendo ancora M. Iseppo Salviati, nobile pittore, data in luce et dedicatami la ... voluta et scrittone di essa assai copiosamente, del quale io so che uno mio amico di sua confessione ne ha tolto copia già molto tempo, et halla lasciata in mano di molti che si fanno inventori di essa." The allusion to the "amico" does not conceal the reference to Palladio, expressed, it seems to me, without the calumnious purpose that ZORZI (1958, p. 126) seems to find.

37 See, for an illuminating piece of information, G. G. ZORZI, 1965, p. 133. He opportunely utilizes, among other things, the testimony of MAGAGNÒ (1610 ed.).

II
THE FRESCOES:
NOTES ON THE ICONOGRAPHY
.AND STYLE

The words that Palladio used to attribute the paintings of Villa Badoer to Giallo Fiorentino are those of praise. He briefly but significantly indicated their type as "grotesques of very beautiful invention."[1] Therefore, he not only knew about the decoration but approved it with words that permit us to associate in a close sequence the dates of the architectural project and the decorative scheme of the rooms. Palladio's words also allow us to hypothesize that the pictorial program was already included in specific terms in the overall design of the villa. The problem of the relationship between architecture and decoration in Palladio is perplexing and intricate, and no claim is being made to confront this problem in all its complexity at this time. For the present purposes it will suffice to bear in mind some conclusions that have been reached in the discussion. At the same time we deny the correctness and functionality of an "interpretive" criticism that emphasizes the intricate richness of the work or that characterizes the kind of discussion that until now has taken place. If the Palladian procedure is to be understood as designing the organization of the space through the filter of a dialectic mediation of the intentions of a certain sphere of patronage—or, to put it another way, if it is to be considered as the expression in formal or aesthetic terms of a type of ideology—then it is not permissible for the architect to absent himself at a crucial moment in the constitutive process of the habitat, the moment, in fact, when the final and clarifying seal is placed on the project. On the

contrary, we know that on some occasions, as at Maser, there was a conflict with the decorators. Such conflicts were caused, however, by a failure to follow the exact directions that were given or by a betrayal of general presuppositions about the correct conception of the ornamentation, not by a systematic program for every decoration on the walls, whether pictorial or plastic. Recently, Forssman,[2] in a polite controversy with Cevese, explained with persuasive arguments the Palladian attitude. In particular he recognized the genesis and the basic principles in the renewed studies of Vitruvius which had been brought about around the beginning of the 1550s by Palladio's meeting with Barbaro. This meeting had given Palladio's Vitruvian studies wider horizons, directing them toward and constituting them into a complete commitment to a restoration of classicism. After having demonstrated that in Palladio's architectonic concept a pictorial program was indispensable, Forssman suggestively hypothesized that Palladio himself may have been, in some cases, the one who ordered the decorations. It is a conjecture that Wolters has not rejected, though he displays caution in regarding it.[3]

A felicitous note by Magagnato offers an important point of departure for a profitable continuation of the discussion. Magagnato emphasizes that in the development of Palladio's designs there is a conscious interplay between the sober, measured, severe "purity" of the exteriors and the decorative richness of the interiors.[4] He stresses that the "correspondence of the whole to the parts, of the parts to each other, and of each to the whole," complicates and enriches.[5] It is, in short, like the dialectic between an absolute and an objective order and can be identified in the rigorous interpretation of the classical norms and the exigencies of suggestive characterization—of individualization. Tafuri's analysis of Palladio's working methods, to which we have referred earlier, is helpful on this point. If it is true that "at the very moment in which Palladio denies to himself his own abstract concept of the style, it is also true that he denies to his patrons the right to claim a projection of their own individual characteristics in the architecture." Thus the Master interprets various requirements of the ruling class as a whole in terms of the imperatives of the design.[6] It is equally true that this permits the inclusion of personal features by means of the "variable" decorative scheme. An "objectivization"—still following Tafuri's analysis[7]—was attained in terms of formal abstraction, thanks to the control of the style of the typology and the general level of the sphere of patronage that formed an ideological superstructure. This restores the possibility of personal identification (obviously not contradictory) between the elements of the decorative scheme, which is controlled by the architect and which postulates a foundation of security and legitimacy. The choice and preference for grotesques, which guided the teams of decorators associated with Palladio between 1550 and 1560,[8] may at first appear surprising or inconsistent when we recall the disapproving statements by Vitruvius that Vasari gathered together.[9] Actually, the grotesques possess a precise logic, to the extent that they do not take on any significance other than that of a decorative instrument, as already described by Cornaro.[10] Also, such decoration may be extrapolated from the world of the Antique and charged with an emblematic value in modern ways determi-

ned by Bramante's Rome, which was thought of as classicism's new Golden Age.[11] The reference points are the discovery of the Golden House of Nero and Raphael's Loggias.[12] The transposition takes place at the end of a dialectic process, with its motivation residing in the secularization of that which is "sacred." This secularization provides the basis for Palladio's typological research which is carried out within the widest context of the ideology of the *renovatio imperii* in which, after Cambrai, the Venetian patrician class found its true being.[13] In stylistic terms the key figures are Raphael, Perin del Vaga, and Giovanni da Udine, whose work is mediated by artists of the Grand Manner and the 'Diaspora, among them the same Giovanni da Udine and Francesco and Giuseppe Salviati.[14] But generally speaking, the grotesques, which in and of themselves were neutral and intended as decoration, allowed room for invention,[15] thereby restoring the possibility of celebrating in allusive sequences the individual characteristics of the patrons.

In the loggia of Villa Badoer, we find a rather conventional parade of grotesque motifs (plates 6,9). On either side of the door, which is surmounted by the Badoer and Loredan family crests[16] (fig. XXI and plate 44), there are two figures of jesters who bow and invite the visitors to enter (fig. XXII). Thus the pictorial image, utilizing an elementary but unequivocal iconographic device, intervenes in the architectonic commentary. It suggests and actually imposes a scenographic interpretation that gives to the stairs its original significance as the "animating element" and restores to the hemicycles all the weight of theatrical allusion. At the same time it establishes the villa (i.e., the rooms of the patrons) as a place of bright invention—a stage on which is celebrated the private spectacle of an intimate and noble myth. The jesters, with their obvious evocation of madness (using the word in Foucault's sense), arouse the suspicion of an unusual performance, one that is charged with capricious and esoteric implications and demands an interpretation of the grotesques displayed inside. Anton Francesco Doni was perhaps right in holding that the "monstrosity" of the individual constitutive elements underlies the structure which is composed of "chimeras and castles in the air wherein are represented with new invention many paintings with fables and histories no longer understood." Doni also wrote, "Because I am not so befuddled that I do not know the representation of Intellect and Madness, the painting of Memory and sculpting of Time, Reform, and the Law, are nothing but castles in the air. But I make them so that I too can join in among these mad ones."[17] In proceeding in this manner we might run the risk of forcing the boundaries of the actual cultural orbit that the decorative program at Fratta expresses. The thesis is also the more open to question since the "jesters" might also represent a vivid memory of the roster of Compagnia della Calza dei Cortesi. Badoer and Giorgio Loredan joined together there in a consortium of "mad ones" intent on expressing themselves through the "madness" of the spectacle,[18] affirming at the same time the friendship which was later to be sealed by kinship. The celebration that is caught and preserved in the pictorial sequence was in fact dedicated to the double bond and was within the perspective of the villa's presence in the reclaimed land that generated it.

An accurate iconographic exegesis of the paintings, on the basis of the present state of knowledge, is impossible. The frescoes clothe the myth in metaphors that employ elements drawn from a literary background which, in its intricacy and its complexity, is perhaps irretrievable, notwithstanding the stimulae of the studies that have been made from Warburg to Saxl, from Seznec to Weise, from Panofsky to Gombrich. It would in any case demand a research in depth and a program out of proportion to the present investigation. It is obvious then that under these conditions a description of the frescoes would be unimportant, if not impertinent. A word, however, can be said in support of the validity of the interpretative key that has been adopted. The pictorial arrangement in the middle room (color plate *b* and plates 46-47) is centered on a nude masculine figure over the entrance to the back garden (color plate *c* and plate 45). The attributes of the figure lead us to see it as a river god and, in observing the desolate background in which it is placed, to identify it as a personification of the Scortico, the Adige, or the Po. In the upper part of the long walls, over the doors leading to the rooms on each side, there are three wide panels of grotesques flanked by female herms. In the lower order there is a high painted socle evoking memories of Vitruvius, as do the many painted profiles around the entrance door.[19] In between the panels with grotesques are four other panels with figures and "histories" which seem to allude to the untamed nature of the site, two more river gods (the Adige, the Po, or the Scortico, plate 65), and the intervention of civilization in the form of Diana and the gods of music (plates 62-64), narrated in episodes whose connective thread is elusive. The paintings in the two large rooms on the left do not present iconographic problems. In substance, they show an obsequiousness to the precepts of Vitruvius in attempting a restoration, almost literally, of Roman fresco decoration. "They began to paint representations of buildings and columns, and to imitate doorways, balconies, and frontispieces...these they adorned with a variety of gardens. They sought also to depict different types of landscapes. Thus they painted ports, promontories, shores, rivers, springs, stretches of water, temples, sacred woods, mountains, sheep, shepherds..."[20] The walls are articulated by painted representations of the architectural orders. In the smaller rooms are pilasters of the Tuscan Order that extend vertically the whole length from the floor to the wooden architraves that support the ceiling (plates 50-51). In the central hall there are half-length engaged Ionic columns that rest on a well-articulated painted socle[21] (plates 48-49). In between the painted architectural features are alternate panels of grotesques and landscapes. The same scheme is followed in the rooms in the right wing. In the room with the Tuscan Order columns, where the Badoer and Loredan coats of arms are displayed over the doors (figs. XIX-XX), these alternate panels display a world of archaeological ruins. In the room with the Ionic columns we see landscapes with architecture (plates 66-69) inspired, at least in the long panels, by obscure historical subjects.[22] Their simple subject matter, noticeable in the flowing, quietly Vitruvian contentment of the frescoes, leads us to think that the two rooms were meant for domestic use, within the general scheme of the practical and ideal functions of the *piano nobile*. This postulation is supported by their position over the kitchens one story below and by the existence in the left wing of the stairway that leads to the ground floor and the granary. The two main rooms in the opposite wing, with their decorations exalting in incredible metaphors the memory of the union between the Badoers and the Loredans, were probably meant for a more private, secluded use, almost as if they served as a temple for meditation and study. The grotesques, which in the lateral rooms surround the two female figures painted over the entranceway to the central hall, have been eliminated here (plate 53). In their place are panels with gods, among whom are numbered Venus surmounted by Pegasus or a Unicorn (plate 55), Minerva

surmounted by Pegasus (plate 54), Bacchus (plate 70) and Vulcan, each dominated by a chariot, Venus and Cupid drawn by two Pegasuses (or Unicorns), and Diana and Apollo surmounted by Centaurs (Chiron? in another panel a goat is seen, perhaps representing Amathea). Two larger panels on the long walls represent episodes of Leda and the Swan (a scene which also appears in a grotesque in the corresponding room in the opposite wing) and the Carrying Off of Ganymede—the culmination of the mythical celebration of the association between Francesco Badoer and Giorgio Loredan and of its unforeseen rupture through the early death of Giorgio (plates 52-53). The representation of the Dioscuri, the sons of Leda, seems to allude to the wish to affirm the origin of the friendship and its fruits as something more than a random happening, since the birth of Castor and Pollux connects the fable with the marriage of the twins to the daughters of Leucippus and since the carrying off of Ganymede is tied to the symbolism of abduction and death (plate 71), though liberated and purified by the reference to Olympus.[23] These two large scenes are the figurative pivot of the pictorial sequence that places the "heroic friendship"[24] on a noble and purified scale. There is little more to say except that the small rooms deeper in the interior are covered with grotesques of a generic type.

Giallo was perhaps summoned to carry out the fresco program because, of the artists grouped around Giuseppe Salviati's workshop, he was the specialist in grotesques (plates 56-61). Salviati's own work of this type is unknown. However, in the stylistic development of the program whose main elements we have attempted to outline, Giallo does not demonstrate the qualities of a painter of great stature. That he was a fresco painter who was capable and very able in his profession is shown by the extent of the work that he could do in one

c. - GIALLO FIORENTINO, *River god (Scortico) on the west wall of the central hall*

day (the amount of wall surface covered with one application of plaster) which, thanks to the restoration, is easily identifiable. But his creative ability is largely determined by powerful cultural influences rather than by the freedom of his own imagination. In the same way the style that articulates and transposes into visual form the concepts and the components of the ornamental decorative scheme reveals a rigidity that is dependent, in vocabulary and in syntax, on the erudite origins and character of the grotesque manner. This rigidity is only rarely redeemed by brief touches of surprising effectiveness (plates 72-73) that look back to the Tuscan-Roman Grand Manner, with some surprising evocations of Michelangelo but without the commitment (in a historic sense) to the Venetian tradition which Salviati was pursuing during those years.[25] The artist thus betrays himself as stylistically *retardataire*. In this sense his work is incompatible with the modernity of the architecture, notwithstanding the fact that it had the approval of Palladio who was as broad-minded in actual practice as he was narrow-minded in theory, limited by his nostalgia for that which was classical and Roman.

NOTES TO CHAPTER II

[1] A. PALLADIO, 1570, L. II, p. 48.

[2] R. CEVESE, 1965, p. 314 (but see also 1967, passim); E. FORSSMAN, 1967, in particular, p. 76.

[3] W. WOLTERS, 1968, pp. 262-263.

[4] L. MAGAGNATO, 1968, pp. 172-173.

[5] A. PALLADIO, 1570, L. I, p. 6; cf. E. FORSSMAN, 1967, p. 71.

[6] M. TAFURI, 1969, p. 124 (and see also E. BATTISTI, 1968, passim).

[7] M. TAFURI, 1969, pp. 123-124.

[8] L. MAGAGNATO, 1968, pp. 170-171 and passim.

[9] VITRUVIUS, VII, 5, 3; "Sed haec, quae ex veris rebus exempla sumebantur, nunc iniquis moribus improbantur. Nam pinguntur tectoriis monstra potius quam ex rebus finitis imagines certae." This corresponds exactly to Vasari's denunciation: "Le grottesche sono una specie di pittura licentiosa e ridicola molto, fatte dagl'antichi per ornamento di vani, dove in alcuni luoghi non stava bene altro che cose in aria."

[10] Cf. in FIOCCO, 1965, p. 167. Cornaro's texts reads: "Quanto allo adornar le sale, et stanzie et loze, io aricordo che siano dipinte, ma non siano di figure si non fossino di mano di gran pittor, perché le figure se non son ben fatte riescono male, ma in luogo di quelle si die pinger paesi, et ancora grotesche, che fano bel vedere; et questo è adornamento di men spesa...," which would lead one to infer a concept of the decoration, as pure decoration, as a background or symbols completely neutral semantically which it is not in practice; see, for example, G. SCHWEIKHART, 1969, pp. 31-62.

[11] L. MAGAGNATO, 1968, pp. 183-184.

[12] For a detailed discussion the recent work by DACOS is fundamental (1969; "introduced" by the fine article of 1966); see also the very lucid and useful contribution of SCHULZ (1965). Cf. also J. BERGSTRÖM, 1957, passim.

[13] M. TAFURI, 1969 (II), pp. 5-6.

[14] Cf., above all, I. CHENEY, 1963, passim.

[15] In light of the illuminating comments of A. and R. PALLUCCHINI (1946) and M. W. ROSKILL (1968) compare the positions of Pino and Dolce, on which C. OSSOLA has recently intervened with a fine study; 1971, pp. 41-49.

[16] The Badoer crest has bands of red and silver, charged with a gold lion rampant. In the Loredan crest the field is divided into gold and blue, each part set with three rosettes, the first arranged in a row and the second scattered.

[17] A. F. DONI, 1564 and 1565, pp. 250 and 248. For proper annotations, cf. C. OSSOLA, 1971, pp. 187-189; for DONI see P. F. GRENDLER, 1965 and 1969. On the iconography of the "grotesque" genre, see F. PIEL, 1962, in particular pp. 47-48, and the rich mine of information in the study by BATTISTI, 1962, especially pp. 304-305. Cf. also E. FORSSMAN, 1956, passim.

[18] A quick identification of the "jesters" with the members of the Calza is certainly unlikely; however, the reference might be only allusive. We know, moreover, the costume of the Cortesi: "La calcia è ... di questi colori: la destra gamba meza di rosasecca, et meza de celeste chiaro, et le costure si giuntano per diritto sul schinco; l'altra tutta di rosato" (ASMo. *Segreto Estense: Cancelleria Estero*. Ambasciatori b. 32: in the dispatch of G. B. Angiari of June 8, 1533). The information of C. VECELLIO (1589, p. 49 v) is, on the contrary, rather general.

[19] A. PALLADIO, 1570, L. I, pp. 55-58.

[20] For the quotation, extracted from Barbaro's version, cf. E. FORSSMAN, 1967, p. 73 (which refers back to VITRUVIUS, VII, 5, 2).

[21] The significance of the use and of the interplay of the two orders should be pursued; for a suggestion, cf. E. FORSSMAN, 1967, p. 76.

[22] For a formulation of the discussion and further cross-references see, on the problem, A. R. TURNER, 1966, passim.

[23] It is more than clear that a discussion, which aims at

going beyond the limits of a mere outline as provided, would have to, first of all, cull the Venetian handbook writing of the first half of the Cinquecento. An examination of the Marcoliniana edition of CARTARI (1556) and of VALERIANO (1556, for some useful points of departure on the personage, cf. G. FIOCCO, 1962) have furnished, as was to be expected, modest results. In any event, from VALERIANO we find that Pegasus is associated with the Muses (p. 32 v) and the Unicorn (if, indeed, the very uncertain identification were to be confirmed) with Valor (pp. 112 and 21).

24 We do not wish here, anachronistically, to recognize a prefiguration of the "amicitis scambievole fra cittadini," theorized in 1623 by Zuccolo (on which, see the very fine study by G. COZZI, 1960, pp. 61-65 and 96-97) in diverse historical circumstances, but nevertheless in a climate prepared in some manner by the situation to which we referred.

25 For a study on the formal characteristics of Venetian decoration around the middle of the Cinquecento, cf. A. BALLARIN, 1968. For our part it is necessary to emphasize the extraneousness of Giallo's grotesques from those of Zelotti, for example, and the stylistic difference (in the dense plasticism, fostered by viscous toned-down colors and characterized by graphic cadences of very manneristic flavor) from those done by decorators near Palladio, such as India and Forbicini.

APPENDIX

I. THE FRESCOES

In the text we have already given a selective description of the frescoes and provided a possible interpretation of the decorative scheme. It will be useful to give here an objective and accurate description of what remains and what has emerged in the recent excellent restoration. At a date not yet determined but certainly before 1750, the frescoes were plastered over. They were long held to be lost, but, after the positive result of the soundings, they have been rediscovered and brought to light by a praiseworthy program initiated by the *Ente Ville Venete* and carried out by the restorers Botter of Treviso. It is unnecessary to point out, since it will soon become obvious, that the difficulties are such as to restrict the exegesis of the paintings to generic observations and that gaps in the identification of the subject matter will appear from time to time. The procedure that follows derives from an arbitrary and convenient selection. To assist the reader we have provided, at the end of this section, a plan of the main floor with the various rooms numbered. References will be made to these numbers below. A specific study of the frescoes is now possible. Such a study will present difficulties, although the key to the enigma seems to us to lie in the allusion celebrating the friendship of Francesco Badoer and Giorgio Loredan within the context of the reclamation of the land.

In the loggia (1) the door leading to the central hall of the *piano nobile* appears overpowered by the united coat of arms of the alliance of Badoer and Loredan. On either side of the door, along the lower and upper parts of the wall, there are panels of grotesques surmounted by festoons. The upper panels of grotesques frame two figures of "jesters" who invite the visitor to enter. On the far sides of the wall are two other panels of grotesques surmounted and framed by festoons. In the area above the secondary entrances to the villa, these panels are repeated on a larger scale and framed by double festoons on the short walls of the loggia. In the central hall (2), above the feigned marble socle on the long walls, triumphal motifs on a yellow ground are alternated with panels of grotesques and framed by herms. There are two mythological components on either side

and one above each of the doors of the small room that face each other. On the left of the entryway there is a group of divinities (Diana, a river nymph, a Muse?). Corresponding to this on the opposite wall there is a pastoral scene centering around Diana. Also on the wall to the left of the entryway is a representation of a pair of male river gods (personifications of the Adige and the Po) which corresponds to another pastoral scene centering around Diana on the opposite wall. The wall with the entryway contains grotesques in the area above the painted socle and in the area on both sides of the door which is surmounted by a painted architrave. On the wall at the other end of the room over the door to the gardens there is a nude figure surrounded by grotesques. The figure may be a personification of the Scortico.

The condition of the frescoes on the whole is quite good, and they can be easily read. The first room on the left where the stairways to the basement and the granary are located (3) was never frescoed. The other small rooms surrounding the central hall (4, 5, 6) contain grotesques painted in a simplified technique, with rapid, almost summary strokes. Here large sections of the paintings have been lost and that which remains is in very bad condition. The back room on the left side (7) is articulated by pilasters of the Tuscan Order that enclose, in the walls without openings, a double register of grotesques crowned with masks. In the areas above the windows there are landscapes. There are also landscapes above the doors, with the exception of the doors leading to the central hall, over which we see the coat of arms of the Badoer family, and the door to the adjoining room, over which we see the coat of arms of the Loredan family.

Room 8 seems enframed by the feigned socle that sustains a series of painted Ionic columns. In the middle of the short walls without openings, there are landscapes surmounted by festoons with masks, while on the "open" walls over the door and window, respectively, there are grotesque fantasies. The decoration on the long walls is complex. The outside wall, like the wall that corresponds to it, has hanging vertical festoons and, over the window, mysterious scenes of two dogs playing and a putto with a kind of swan. In the central section above the fireplace

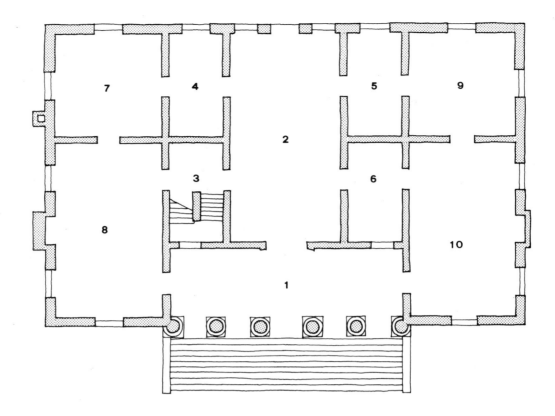

is a landscape guarded by mythological divinities and by a double festoon with masks. The internal wall has a landscape in the middle and panels of grotesques. The condition of the paintings in both rooms is on the whole satisfactory. The condition of the grotesques on the fourth wall of the back room on the right side (9) is, however, such as to render any description useless except for the two female figures over the door to room 10. Room 10, as we have emphasized in the text, provides the key decorations. The lower zone of the whole room is covered by a feigned marble base. On the short wall with the door, the upper register represents Juno, Venus, and Mars. On the other short wall there are three other deities in landscapes above the window. Minerva

and Venus surmounted by Pegasus on one side, and Diana and Apollo surmounted by Centaurs on the other, flank the central images. The middle of the long walls are occupied by two large panels. On the right are Leda, the Swan, and the Dioscuri and three panels containing a satyr, an infant satyr, and a goat (Amalthea?). The long wall on the opposite side contains a scene relating to the myth of the Dioscuri, "enframed" by the representations which link it to the divine epiphany of the short walls. In one there is a representation of Bacchus surmounted by a chariot carrying Venus and triumph and pulled by Pegasus. In the other is a scene of Vulcan surmounted by a chariot carrying Cupid, also pulled by Pegasus.

II. Comparable Table of the Measurements Given by Palladio, Bertotti Scamozzi, and C.I.S.A.

Plans	Length (meters)	Width (meters)
Loggia		
Palladio	12.14	4.16
Bertotti	11.72	3.99
C.I.S.A.	12.05	3.99
Rooms on the southeast and northwest sides		
Palladio	5.55	9.19
Bertotti	5.65	9.40
C.I.S.A.	5.72	9.57
The central hall		
Palladio	5.55	11.10
Bertotti	5.55	11.03
C.I.S.A.	5.75	11.33
The stairwell and the room corresponding to it on the right		
Palladio	2.77	—
Bertotti	2.77	4.89
C.I.S.A.	2.89	5.40
The inner chambers that face the rear and flank the central hall		
Palladio	2.77	5.55
Bertotti	2.77	5.55
C.I.S.A.	2.87	5.68
The smaller rooms at the southwest and northwest corners		
Palladio	2.77	5.55
Bertotti	2.77	5.55
C.I.S.A.	2.87	5.68

Depth of the lateral colonnades (meters)

Palladio   4.85
Bertotti   4.47
C.I.S.A.   4.47 left — 4.31 right

Depth of the buildings behind the colonnades (meters)

Palladio   6.94
Bertotti   7.04
C.I.S.A.   7.29 left — 7.21 right

Intercolumniation of the colonnade (meters)

Palladio   2.77
Bertotti   2.70
C.I.S.A.   left   from 2.59 to 2.65
                         right from 2.43 to 2.58

Elevations	Height (meters)	Cornice (meters)
The walls between the socle and the cornice		
Palladio	6.94	1.38
Bertotti	6.80	1.66
C.I.S.A.	6.93	1.34
The columns of the lateral colonnade		
Palladio	4.85	—
Bertotti	4.82	—
C.I.S.A.	4.93	—

BIBLIOGRAPHY

I) MANUSCRIPT SOURCES

M. BARBARO, *Arbori de Patritii Veneti*. Cod. Miscellanea Veneta I. Storia Veneta, ASV.

M. BARBARO, *Discendenze patrizie*. Cod. Consultaz. XI-E-2, BCV.

M. BARBARO, *Famiglie nobili Venete*. Cod. 6155, ÖNB.

M. BARBARO, *Nozze*. Cod. It. VII, 156 (= 8492), BMV.

A. C. BELLETTATO, *Villa Badoer detta "La Badoera" di Fratta Polesine*, 1967, CISA.

M. A. CAMPANELLA, *Delle iscrizioni pubbliche e private, sacre e profane ... del Polesine di Rovigo di quelle di questa città e borghi*. Part I, 1750, ms. Silv. 486, BCR.

G. A. CAPPELLARI VIVARO, *Il Campidoglio Veneto*. Cod. It. VII, 15-16 (= 8304-8305), BMV.

A. F. DONI, *Attavanta*, ca. 1555. Ms. 1433, BCV.

G. FOLCO PIZZO, *Sante Baseggio*. Degree thesis at the Istituto di Storia dell'Arte of the University of Padua (with C. Semenzato), 1970.

Indice di tutte le parti più notabili che sono nei Libri della Comunità. Ms. Silv. 619, BCR.

Nascimento de Nobili veneziani. Cod. It. VII, 173 (= 8160), BMV.

Necrologio de' nobili veneziani dal 1530 al 1613. Cod. It. VII, 353, BMV.

[G. PRIULI,] *Pretiosi Frutti del Maggior Consiglio ... sino al presente anno MDCXIX*. Cod. Cicogna 5781, BCV.

B. RIGOBELLO, *Origini del Retratto della Vespara*, 1967, ACL.

G. SILVESTRI, *Storia agraria del Polesine di Rovigo*. Ms. Silv. 446-449, BCR.

G. SILVESTRI, *Copie o transunti del Memoriale manoscritto delle cose occorrenti in Rovigo di Giovanni Campo* [1560-1570], 1756. Ms. Silv. 715, BCR.

G. SILVESTRI, *Giornale storico delle cose rimarcabili che ... accadono in Rovigo e nel Polesine tutto ... dall'anno MDCCXL* [1755-1756]. Ms. Silv. 321, BCR.

II) PRINTED WORKS

1496-1533 M. SANUDO, *Diari* (ed. Venice, 1897-1902).

1499-1540 R. DI SPILIMBERGO, *Cronaca de' suoi tempi dal 1499 al 1540* [edited by V. Ioppi, Udine, 1884].

1548 P. PINO, *Dialogo di pittura*, Venezia [edited by A. and R. Pallucchini, Venice, 1946].

1552 G. PORTA, *Regola di far perfettamente col compasso la voluta*, Venice.

1554 A. PALLADIO, *L'Antichità di Roma*, Rome.

1555 A. F. DONI, *Seconda Libraria*, Venice.

1556 D. BARBARO, *I Dieci Libri dell'Architettura di M. Vitruvio tradotti et commentati*, Venice.

1556 V. CARTARI, *Le imagini con la sposizione de i Dei de gli Antichi*, Venice.

1556 F. DA LONGIANO, *Del modo di tradurre*, Venice.

1556 P. VALERIANO, *Hieroglyphica sive de sacris Aegyptiorum litteris commentarii*, Basilea.

1557 D. BARBARO, *Dell'eloquenza*, Venice.

1564 A. F. DONI, *Le Pitture*, Padua.

1565 A. F. DONI, *La Zucca*, Venice.

1565 A. F. DONI (II), *Le Ville*, Bologna.

1567 D. BARBARO, *I Dieci Libri dell'Architettura tradotti et commentati*, Venice.

1568 G. VASARI, *Le Vite*, Florence [edited by G. Milanesi, Florence, 1906].

1570 A. PALLADIO, *I Quattro Libri dell'Architettura*, Venice.

1581 F. SANSOVINO, *Venetia città nobilissima et singolare*, Venice.

1583 V. SCAMOZZI, *Discorsi sopra le antichità di Roma*, Venice.

1589 C. VECELLIO, *Habiti antichi et moderni di tutto il mondo*, Venice.

1590 N. FRANCO, *Dialoghi piacevolissimi*, Venice.

1604 F. SANSOVINO, *Venetia città nobilissima et singolare ... ampliata* dal M. R. D. GIOVANNI STRINGA, Venice.

1609 P. ARETINO, *Il secondo libro de le lettere*, vol. I, Paris.

1610 MAGAGNÒ [MENON e BEGOTTO], *Rime rustiche*, Venice.

1615 V. SCAMOZZI, *L'Idea dell'Architettura Universale*, Venice.

1617 P. GUALDO, "Vita di Andrea Palladio" [edited by G. G. Zorzi, in *Saggi e Memorie di Storia dell'Arte*, 1958-1959, pp. 93-104].

1618 C. RIPA, *Nuova Iconologia*, Padua.

1634 G. B. BARPO, *Le delitie e i frutti dell'agricoltura e della villa*, Venice.

1648 C. RIDOLFI, *Le Maraviglie dell'Arte*, Venice [edited by D. v. Hadeln, Berlin, 1914-1924].

1658 A. ZEN, *Il cavallo di razza riconosciuto dal segno de' marchi*, Venice.

1663 F. SANSOVINO, *Venetia città nobilissima et singolare ... con nove e copiose aggiunte di D.* GIUSTINIAN MARTINIONI, Venice.

1681 G. AGOSTINETTI, *Cento e dieci modi che formano il buon fattore di villa*, Venice.

1715 G. LEONI, *L'Architettura di Andrea Palladio in inglese, italiano e francese, con note ed osservazioni di* INNICO JONES, *riveduta, disegnata e pubblicata*, London.

1721 G. LEONI, *The Architecture of A. Palladio in Four Books ... Translated from the Italian Original*, II, London.

1738 I. WARE, *The Four Books of Andrea Palladio's Architecture*, II, London.

1740 [F. MUTTONI], *Architettura di Andrea Palladio Vicentino di nuovo ristampata ... con le osservazioni dell'architetto N. N.*, I, Venice.

1744 [F. MUTTONI], *Architettura di Andrea Palladio Vicentino di nuovo ristampata ... con le osservazioni dell'architetto N. N.*, V, Venice.

1748 G. G. BRONZIERO, *Istoria delle origini e condizioni de' luoghi principali del Polesine di Rovigo*, Venice.

1778 T. TEMANZA, *Vite dei più celebri architetti veneziani*, Venice [edited by L. Grassi, Milan, 1966].

1781 O. BERTOTTI SCAMOZZI, *Le Fabbriche e i Disegni di Andrea Palladio*, III, Vicenza.

1785 F. MILIZIA, *Memorie degli architetti antichi e moderni*, vol. 2, Bassano [cited from 1827 edition, Bologna].

1791 A. MUCCI, *I Quattro Libri dell'Architettura di Andrea Palladio*, Siena.

1810 L. CICOGNARA, *Elogio di Andrea Palladio*, Venice.

1814 G. B. VERCI, *Storia degli Eccelini*, vol. II, Venice.

1817 A. DIEDO, *Elogio di Daniele Barbaro*, Venice.

1824-1853 E. A. CICOGNA, *Delle Inscrizioni Veneziane*, vol. 6, Venice.

1830 A. C. QUATREMÈRE DE QUINCY, *Histoire de la vie et des ouvrages des plus célèbres architects*, vol. II, Paris

1845 A. MAGRINI, *Memorie intorno la vita e le opere di Andrea Palladio*, Padua.

1847 A. MAGRINI, *Il Teatro Olimpico*, Padua.

1852 B. GONZATI, *La Basilica di S. Antonio di Padova*, vol. 2, Padua.

1852 P. PARUTA, *Opere politiche*, vol. I, Florence.

1857 A. F. DONI, *Attavanta*, Florence.

1865 G. DURAZZO, *Dei Rettori Veneziani in Rovigo*, Venice.

1865 G. I. FONTANA, *Cento palazzi fra i più celebri di Venezia*, Venice.

1868 G. LORENZI, *Monumenti per servire alla storia del Palazzo Ducale di Venezia*, Venice.

1874 C. YRIARTE, *La vie d'un patricien de Venise au seizième siècle*, vol. 2, Paris.

1879 [1880] F. A. BOCCHI, *Trattato geografico-economico comparativo per servire alla storia dell'antica Adria e del Polesine di Rovigo*, Adria.

1880 L. FERRARI, *Palladio e Venezia*, Venice.

1884 V. JOPPI, see R. DI SPILIMBERGO, 1499-1540.

1888 J. W. BRADLEY, *Dictionary of Miniaturist, Illuminators, Calligraphers and Copyists*, vol. II, London.

1890 G. NICOLETTI, "Lista di nomi di artisti tolta dai libri di tanse e luminarie della Fraglia dei Pittori," in *Ateneo Veneto*, p. 378.

1901 R. BROTTI, "Miniatori veneziani," in *Nuovo Archivio Veneto*, p. 70.

1902 F. BANISTER-FLETCHER, *Andrea Palladio, His Life and Works*, London.

1906 G. MILANESI, see G. VASARI, 1568.

1909 See *Bernieri Antonio*, in THIEME BECKER, *Künstler Lexikon*, vol. III, Leipzig, p. 459.

1909 F. BURGER, *Die Villen des Andrea Palladio*, Leipzig.

1909 W. HEINEMANN, *Die Villenbauten des Andrea Palladio*, Berlin.

1909 L. VENTURI, *Le Compagnie della Calza (sec. XV, XVI)*, Venice.

1911 D. v. HADELN, "Nachrichten über Miniaturmaler," in *AA. VV., Archivalische Beitrage zur Geschichte der Venezianischen Kunst*, Berlin.

1914 G. GURLITT, *Andrea Palladio*, Berlin.

1914 D. v. HADELN, see C. RIDOLFI, 1648.

1925 A. CAPPELLINI, *Il Polesine*, Rovigo.

1926 G. K. LOUKOMSKI, *Les Villas des Doges de Venise*, vol. 2, Paris.

1927 G. K. LOUKOMSKI, *Andrea Palladio, sa vie, son oeuvre*, Paris.

1927 U. MOZZI, *I Magistrati veneti alle Acque e alle Bonifiche*, Bologna.

1928 G. M. CANTACUZÈNE, *Palladio. Essai critique*, Bucharest.

1928 A. MELANI, *Palladio (1508-1580), la sua vita, la sua arte, le sue influenze*, Milan.

1930 G. C. ARGAN, "Palladio e la critica neoclassica," in *L'Arte*, pp. 327-346.

1932 R. ALMAGIÀ, "Gastaldi Giacomo (o Jacopo)," in *Enciclopedia Italiana*, vol. XVI, Milan, p. 430.

1933 P. S. LEICHT, "Ideali di vita dei Veneziani del Cinquecento," in *Archivio Veneto*, pp. 217-231.

1933 H. TIETZE, "Eugenio di Savoia, amico dell'arte," in *Le vie d'Italia e del Mondo*, pp. 891-907.

1936 R. CESSI, "Alvise Cornaro e la bonifica veneziana nel secolo XVI," in *Rendiconti della R. Accademia dei Lincei*, pp. 301-323.

1936 L. FOSCARI, *Affreschi esterni a Venezia*, Milan.

1937 E. CAMPOS, *I Consorzi di Bonifica nella Repubblica Veneta*, Padua.

1937 V. MARPILLERO, "L'opera di G. da Udine nel Palazzo Grimani di S. Maria Formosa," in *Le Panarie*.

1940 A. VENTURI, *Storia dell'arte italiana. Architettura del Cinquecento*, vol. XI, Part 3, Milan.

1941 A. CAPPELLINI, "Castelli scomparsi e avanzi di castelli nel Polesine," in *Bollettino dell'Istituto Storico e di Cultura dell'Arma del Genio*, fasc. 14.

1941 R. CESSI, see G. PRIULI, 1941.

1941 F. FRANCO, "Classicismo e funzionalità della villa palladiana 'città picciola,'" in *Atti del I Congresso Nazionale di Storia dell'Architettura* [1936], Rome, p. 6.

1941 G. PRIULI, "I diari," in *Rerum Italicarum Scriptores*, Bologna, vol. IV, pp. 31-58.

1941 M. F. TURRINI, *Bonifiche polesane*, Rovigo.

1943 A. M. DALLA POZZA, *Andrea Palladio*, Vicenza.

1946 A. and R. PALLUCCHINI, see P. PINO, 1548.

1949 S. BETTINI, "La critica dell'architettura e l'arte di Palladio," in *Arte Veneta*, pp. 55-69.

1949 V. LAZZARINI, "Beni carraresi e proprietari veneziani," in *Studi in onore di Gino Luzzato*, vol. I, Milan, pp. 474-488.

1950 R. PALLUCCHINI, *La giovinezza del Tintoretto*, Milan.

1952 F. BARBIERI, *Vincenzo Scamozzi*, Vicenza.

1953 F. BRAUDEL, *Civiltà e imperi del Mediterraneo nell'età di Filippo II*, Turin.

1954 G. MARCHIORI, "Ville della Provincia di Rovigo," in *AA. VV., Le Ville Venete*, Treviso.

1954 M. MURARO, *Les Villas de la Venetie*, Venice.

1954 R. WITTKOWER, "Giacomo Leoni's edition of Palladio's 'Quattro Libri dell'Architettura,'" in *Arte Veneta*, pp. 310-316.

1954 G. G. ZORZI, "Progetti giovanili di Andrea Palladio per villini e case di campagna," in *Palladio*, pp. 105-121.

1955 M. BERENGO, *La società veneta alla fine del '700*, Florence.

1955 R. GALLO, "Andrea Palladio e Venezia," in *Rivista di Venezia*, pp. 23-48.

1955 G. MASSON, "Palladian Villas as rural center," in *The Architectural Review*, pp. 17-20.

1956 G. C. ARGAN, "L'importanza del Sanmicheli nella formazione del Palladio," in *Venezia e l'Europa. Atti del XVIII Congresso Internazionale di Storia dell'Arte*, Venice, pp. 387-389.

1956 E. FORSSMAN, *Säule und Ornament*, Stockholm.

1956 F. FRANCO, "Piccola urbanistica della 'casa di villa' palladiana," in *Venezia e l'Europa. Atti del XVIII Congresso Internazionale di Storia dell'Arte*, Venice, pp. 395-398.

1956 R. GALLO, "Andrea Palladio e Venezia. Di alcuni edifici ignoti o mal noti," in *Venezia e l'Europa. Atti del XVIII Congresso Internazionale di Storia dell'Arte*, Venice, pp. 398-402.

1956 G. LORENZETTI, *Venezia e il suo Estuario*, Rome.

1956 R. PANE, "Andrea Palladio e l'interpretazione dell'architettura rinascimentale," in *Venezia e l'Europa. Atti del XVIII Congresso Internazionale di Storia dell'Arte*, Venice, pp. 408-412.

1957 J. S. ACKERMAN, "The Belvedere as a Classical Villa," in *Journal of the Warburg and Courtauld Institutes*, p. 70.

1957 J. BERGSTRÖM, "Revival of antique illusionistic Wall Painting," in *Renaissance Art*, Göteborg.

1957 A. SERPIERI, *Le bonifiche nella storia e nella dottrina*, Bologna.

1957-1960 P. ARETINO, *Lettere sull'arte*, vol. 4 [edited by F. Pertile and E. Camesasca], Milan.

1957-1960 F. PERTILE and E. CAMESASCA, see P. ARETINO, 1957-1960.

1958 F. BRAUDEL, "La vita economica di Venezia nel secolo XVI," in AA. VV., *La civiltà veneziana del Cinquecento*, Florence, pp. 29-55.

1958 R. PALLUCCHINI, "Giulio Romano e Palladio," in *Arte Veneta*, pp. 234-235.

1958 G. G. ZORZI, *I disegni delle antichità di Andrea Palladio*, Venice.

1958-1959 G. G. ZORZI, see P. GUALDO, 1617.

1959 G. C. ARGAN, "Tipologia, simbologia, allegorismo delle forme architettoniche," in *Bollettino del Centro Internazionale di Studi di Architettura di A. Palladio*, Vicenza, I, pp. 13-16.

1959 F. FRANCO, "Piccola e grande urbanistica palladiana," in *Bollettino del Centro Internazionale di Studi di Architettura A. Palladio*, Vicenza, I, pp. 17-20.

1959 A. HAMBERG, "The Villa of Lorenzo il Magnifico at Poggio a Caiano and the Origin of Palladianism," in *Figura*, p. 76.

1959 R. PALLUCCHINI, "Andrea Palladio e Giulio Romano," in *Bollettino del Centro Internazionale di Studi di Architettura A. Palladio*, Vicenza, I, pp. 36-44.

1959 R. PANE, "La formazione del Palladio e il Manierismo," in *Bollettino del Centro Internazionale di Studi di Architettura A. Palladio*, Vicenza, I, pp. 48-50.

1959 W. REARICK, "Battista Franco and the Grimani Chapel," in *Saggi e Memorie di Storia dell'Arte*, pp. 107-139.

1960 A. CHASTEL, "Palladio e l'escalier à double mouvement inversé," in *Bollettino del Centro Internazionale di Studi di Architettura A. Palladio*, Vicenza, I, pp. 26-29.

1960 A. CHASTEL (II), "Palladio et l'art des fêtes," in *Bollettino del Centro Internazionale di Studi di Architettura A. Palladio*, Vicenza, II, pp. 29-33.

1960 D. R. COFFIN, *The Villa d'Este at Tivoli*, Princeton.

1960 G. COZZI, "Una vicenda nella Venezia barocca: Marco Trevisan e la sua 'eroica amicizia,'" in *Bollettino di Storia della Società e dello Stato Veneziano*, pp. 61-154.

1960 R. GALLO, "Sanmicheli a Venezia," in AA.VV., *Michele Sanmicheli*, Verona.

1960 V. LAZZARINI, *Proprietà e feudi in antiche carte veneziane*, Rome.

1960 M. ZOCCA, "Le concezioni urbanistiche di Palladio," in *Palladio*, pp. 67-83.

1960 G. G. ZORZI, "Andrea Palladio architetto della Repubblica di Venezia," in *Bollettino del Centro Internazionale di Studi di Architettura A. Palladio*, Vicenza, II, pp. 108-113.

1961 D. BELTRAMI, *La penetrazione economica dei Veneziani in terraferma. Forze di lavoro e proprietà fondiaria nelle campagne venete dei secoli XVII e XVIII*, Venice-Rome.

1961 S. BETTINI, "Palladio urbanista," in *Arte Veneta*, pp. 89-98.

1961 S. BETTINI (II), "Palladio urbanista," in *Bollettino del Centro Internazionale di Studi di Architettura A. Palladio*, Vicenza, III, pp. 89-91.

1961 G. LUZZATO, *Storia economica di Venezia dall'XI al XVI secolo*, Venice.

1961 R. PALLUCCHINI, "Andrea Palladio e Giulio Romano," in *Bollettino del Centro Internazionale di Studi di Architettura A. Palladio*, Vicenza, III, pp. 38-44.

1961 R. PANE, *Andrea Palladio*, Turin.

1961 J. SCHULZ, "Vasari at Venice," in *The Burlington Magazine*, pp. 500-511.

1961 R. WITTKOWER, "Sviluppo stilistico dell'architettura palladiana," in *Bollettino del Centro Internazionale di Studi di Architettura A. Palladio*, Vicenza, III, pp. 61-65.

1961 G. G. ZORZI, "Errori, deficienze e inesattezze de 'I Quattro Libri dell'Architettura' di A. Palladio," in *Bollettino del Centro Internazionale di Studi di Architettura A. Palladio*, Vicenza, III, pp. 143-148.

1961 G. G. ZORZI (II), "I disegni delle opere palladiane pubblicate su 'I Quattro Libri' e il loro significato rispetto alle opere eseguite," in *Bollettino del Centro Internazionale di Studi di Architettura A. Palladio*, Vicenza, III, pp. 12-17.

1962 E. BATTISTI, *L'Antirinascimento*, Milan.

1962 L. CROSATO, *Gli affreschi nelle ville venete del Cinquecento*, Treviso.

1962 G. FIOCCO, "Il ritratto di Pietro Valeriano," in *Archivio Storico di Belluno, Feltre e Cadore*, pp. 1-6.

1962 E. FORSSMAN, "Palladio e Vitruvio," in *Bollettino del Centro Internazionale di Studi di Architettura A. Palladio*, Vicenza, IV, pp. 31-42.

1962 M. LEVI D'ANCONA, "Jacopo del Giallo e alcune miniature del Correr," in *Bollettino dei Musei Civici Veneziani*, 2, pp. 1-23.

1962 M. LEVI D'ANCONA (II), *Miniatura e miniatori a Firenze dal XIV al XVI secolo*, Florence.

1962 W. LOTZ, "La Rotonda: edificio civile con cupola," in *Bollettino del Centro Internazionale di Studi di Architettura A. Palladio*, Vicenza, IV, p. 69.

1962 G. MAZZOTTI, "Le Ville venete e l'opera dell'Ente istituito per il loro restauro e conservazione," in *Giornale Economico della Camera di Commercio, Industria e Agricoltura di Vicenza*, pp. 817-826.

1962 M. MURARO, *Venetian Treasures*, Geneva.

1962 P. PASCHINI, "Daniele Barbaro letterato e prelato veneziano nel Cinquecento," in *Rivista di Storia della Chiesa in Italia*, pp. 73-107.

1962 F. PIEL, *Die Ornament-Groteske in der italienischen Renaissance*, Berlin.

1962 E. SERENI, *Storia del paesaggio agrario in Italia*, Bari.

1962 R. WITTKOWER, *Principi architettonici nell'età dell'umanesimo* [1949], Turin.

1962 S. J. WOOLF, "Venice and Terraferma. Problems of the change from commercial to the landed activities," in *Bollettino dell'Istituto di Storia della Società e dello Stato Veneziano*, pp. 415-441.

1963 R. ASSUNTO, "Introduzione alla critica del paesaggio," in *De homine*, p. 254.

1963 S. BOTTARI, "I Quattro libri dell'Architettura," in *Bollettino del Centro Internazionale di Studi di Architettura A. Palladio*, Vicenza, V, pp. 24-32.

1963 I. CHENEY, "Francesco Salviati's North Italian Journey," in *The Art Bulletin*, pp. 337-349.

1963 G. FIOCCO, "La lezione di Alvise Cornaro," in *Bollettino del Centro Internazionale di Studi di Architettura A. Palladio*, Vicenza, V, pp. 33-43.

1963 M. HIRST, "Three Ceiling Decorations by Francesco Salviati," in *Zeitschrift für Kungstgeschichte*, pp. 146-165.

1963 E. MANDOWSKY - CH. MITCHELL, *Pirro Ligorio's Roman Antiquities*, London.

1963 G. MAZZOTTI, *Ville Venete*, Rome.

1963 G. PIOVENE, "Trissino e Palladio nell'Umanesimo vicentino," in *Bollettino del Centro Internazionale di Studi di Architettura A. Palladio*, Vicenza, V, pp. 13-23.

1963 L. Puppi, *Il Teatro Olimpico*, Venice.

1963 B. Rupprecht, "Die Villa Garzoni des Jacopo Sansovino," in *Mitteilungen des Kunsthistorischen Institutes in Florenz*, pp. 4-32.

1963 B. Zevi, "Palladio," in *Enciclopedia Universale dell'Arte*, vol. X, cll. 438-458.

1964 M. Baratto, *Tre saggi sul teatro*, Venice.

1964 F. Barbieri, "Palladio e il Manierismo," in *Bollettino del Centro Internazionale di Studi di Architettura A. Palladio*, Vicenza, VI, pp. 49-63.

1964 A. De Maddalena, "Il mondo rurale italiano nel Cinquecento e nel Seicento (Rassegna di studi recenti)," in *Rivista Storica Italiana*, pp. 348-426.

1964 M. Guiotto, "Recenti restauri di edifici palladiani," in *Bollettino del Centro Internazionale di Studi di Architettura A. Palladio*, Vicenza, VI, pp. 70-88.

1964 R. Pane, "Palladio e la moderna storiografia dell'architettura," in *Bollettino del Centro Internazionale di Studi di Architettura A. Palladio*, Vicenza, VI, pp. 119-130.

1964 B. Rigobello, *Un antico consorzio di bonifica veneto*, Venice.

1964 B. Rupprecht, "Ville Venete del '400 e del primo '500: forme e sviluppo," in *Bollettino del Centro Internazionale di Studi di Architettura A. Palladio*, Vicenza, VI, pp. 239-250.

1964 A. Ventura, *Nobiltà e popolo nella società veneta del '400 e '500*, Bari.

1964 B. Zevi, "Michelangiolo e Palladio," in *Bollettino del Centro Internazionale di Studi di Architettura A. Palladio*, Vicenza, VI, pp. 13-28.

1964 L. Zorzi, "La scena veneta prima del Palladio," in *Comunità*, pp. 40-57.

1964-1965 A. M. Dalla Pozza, "Palladiana X-XI-XII," in *Odeo Olimpico*, pp. 203-238.

1965 P. Bieganski, "I problemi della composozione spaziale delle ville palladiane," in *Bollettino del Centro Internazionale di Studi di Architettura A. Palladio*, Vicenza, VI, pp. 23-24.

1965 R. Cevese, "Appunti palladiani," in *Bollettino del Centro Internazionale di Studi di Architettura A. Palladio*, Vicenza, VII, pp. 305-315.

1965 A. Chastel, "Palladio et l'escalier," in *Bollettino del Centro Internazionale di Studi di Architettura A. Palladio*, Vicenza, VII, pp. 11-22.

1965 A. M. Dalla Pozza, "Elementi e motivi ricorrenti in A. Palladio," in *Bollettino del Centro Internazionale di Studi di Architettura A. Palladio*, Vicenza, VII, pp. 43-58.

1965 G. Fiocco, *Alvise Cornaro. Il suo tempo e le sue opere*, Venice.

1965 E. Forssman, *Palladios Lehrgebäude*, Uppsala.

1965 P. F. Grendler, "Utopia in Renaissance: Doni's 'New World,'" in *Journal of the History of Ideas*, p. 479-494.

1965 A. Niero, "Documenti sulla Scuola dei Dipintori," in *Arte Veneta*, pp. 138-141.

1965 T. Pignatti, "La Farglia dei pittori di Venezia," in *Bollettino dei Musei Civici Veneziani*, 3, pp. 16-39.

1965 L. Polacco, "La posizione di Palladio di fronte all'antichità," in *Bollettino del Centro Internazionale di Studi di Architettura A. Palladio*, Vicenza, VII, pp. 59-76.

1965 J. Schulz, "Pinturicchio and the Revival of Antiquity," in *Journal of the Warburg and Courtauld Institutes*, pp. 35-55.

1965 G. G. Zorzi, *Le opere pubbliche e i palazzi privati di Andrea Palladio*, Vicenza.

1965-1966 L. Puppi, "Appunti su Villa Badoer di Fratta Polesine," in *Memorie dell'Accademia Patavina di SS.LL.AA.*, pp. 47-72.

1966 J. S. Ackerman, *Palladio*, Harmondsworth.

1966 N. Dacos, "Per la storia delle grottesche," in *Bollettino d'Arte*, p. 43.

1966 E. Forssman, "Palladio e Daniele Barbaro," in *Bollettino del Centro Internazionale di Studi di Architettura A. Palladio*, Vicenza, VIII, pp. 68-81.

1966 E. Forssman (II), "Falconetto e Palladio," in *Bollettino del Centro Internazionale di Studi di Architettura A. Palladio*, pp. 52-67.

1966 J. J. Gloton, "La villa italienne à la fin de la Renaissance. Conceptions palladiennes - conceptians vignolesques," in *Bollettino del Centro Internazionale di Studi di Architettura A. Palladio*, Vicenza, VIII, pp. 101-113.

1966 L. Grassi, see T. Temanza, 1778.

1966 M. Muraro, "Civiltà delle ville venete," in *Arte in Europa. Scritti di Storia dell'Arte in onore di E. Arslan*, Milan.

1966 L. Padoan Urban, "Teatri e 'Teatri del mondo' nella Venezia del Cinquecento," in *Arte Veneta*, pp. 137-146.

1966 L. Puppi, *Palladio*, Florence.

1966 M. Rosci, *Il trattato di architettura di Sebastiano Serlio*, Milan.

1966 M. Rosci (II), "Schemi di ville nel VII libro del Serlio e ville palladiane," in *Bollettino del Centro Internazionale di Studi di Architettura A. Palladio*, Vicenza, VIII, pp. 128-133.

1966 B. Rupprecht, "Villa. Zur Geschichte eines Ideals," in *AA.VV., Probleme der Kunstwissenschaft*, vol. II, Berlin, pp. 210-250.

1966 H. Spielmann, *Andrea Palladio und die Antike*, Munich-Berlin.

1966 M. Tafuri, *L'architettura del Manierismo nel '500 europeo*, Rome.

1966 A. R. Turner, *The Vision of Landscape in Renaissance Italy*, Princeton.

1967 J. S. Ackerman, *Palladio's Villas*, Glückstadt.

1967 A. Ballarin, "Jacopo Bassano e lo studio di Raffaello e dei Salviati," in *Arte Veneta*, pp. 77-101.

1967 R. Cevese, "Proposta per una nuova lettura critica dell'arte palladiana," in *Essays in the History of Architecture presented to Rudolf Wittkower*, London, pp. 122-127.

1967 G. Cherubini, "Qualche considerazione sulle campagne dell'Italia settentrionale tra l'XI e il XV secolo (in margine alle ricerche di Elio Conti)," in *Rivista Storica Italiana*, p. 112.

1967 D. R. Coffin, "The plans of the Villa Madama," in *The Art Bulletin*, p. 111.

1967 G. Faggin, "Il mondo culturale veneto del Cinquecento e Andrea Palladio," in *Bollettino del Centro Internazionale di Studi di Architettura A. Palladio*, Vicenza, IX, pp. 49-65.

1967 G. I. Fontana, *Venezia monumentale: i Palazzi* [edited by L. Moretti], Venice.

1967 E. Forssman, "Palladio e la pittura a fresco," in *Arte Veneta*, pp. 71-76.

1967 P. Foster, "Raphael on the Villa Madama: the text of a lost letter," in *Römisches Jahrbuch für Kunstgeschichte*, p. 307.

1967 E. Garin, *La cultura del Rinascimento*, Bari.

1967 N. Ivanoff, *Palladio*, Milan.

1967 G. Mazzotti, *Ville Venete*, Rome.

1967 M. Muraro, "Concretezza e idealità nell'arte del Palladio," in *Bollettino del Centro Internazionale di Studi di Architettura A. Palladio*, Vicenza, IX, p. 108.

1967 C. Rowe, "The Mathematics of the Ideal Villa. Palladio and Le Corbusier compared," in *The Architectural Review*, p. 101.

1967 C. Semenzato, "Gli spazi esterni e il manierismo di Andrea Palladio," in *Bollettino del Centro Internazionale di Studi di Architettura A. Palladio*, Vicenza, I, pp. 342-353.

1967 R. Zangheri, "Gli studi di storia dell'agricoltura nell'ultimo ventennio," in *Studi Storici*, pp. 668-695.

1968 A. Ballarin, "La decorazione ad affresco della villa veneta nel quinto decennio del Cinquecento," in *Bollettino del*

Centro Internazionale di Studi di Architettura A. Palladio, Vicenza, X, pp. 115-126.

1968   E. BATTISTI, "Le tendenze all'unità verso la metà del Cinquecento," in *Bollettino del Centro Internazionale di Studi di Architettura A. Palladio,* Vicenza, X, p. 127.

1968   P. BIEGANSKI, "La struttura architettonica di alcune ville di Palladio in rapporto alla loro funzione pratica," in *Bollettino del Centro Internazionale di Studi di Architettura A. Palladio,* Vicenza, X, pp. 15-30.

1968   G. FERRARA, *Architettura del paesaggio italiano,* Padua.

1968   L. MAGAGNATO, "I collaboratori veronesi di Andrea Palladio," in *Bollettino del Centro Internazionale di Studi di Architettura A. Palladio,* Vicenza, X, pp. 170-187.

1968   B. PULLAN, *Crisis and Change in the Venetian economy in the 16th and 17th centuries,* London.

1968   M. W. ROSKILL, *Dolce's "Aretino" and Venetian Art Theory of the Cinquecento,* New York.

1968   M. ROSCI, "Forme e funzioni delle ville venete prepalladiane," in *L'Arte,* 2, pp. 27-54.

1968   B. RUPPRECHT, "L'iconologia nella villa veneta," in *Bollettino del Centro Internazionale di Studi di Architettura A. Palladio,* Vicenza, X, pp. 229-240.

1968   B. RUPPRECHT (II), "Sanmichelis Villa Soranza," in *Festschrift Ulrich Middeldorf,* Berlin.

1968   M. TAFURI, "Teatro e città nell'architettura palladiana," in *Bollettino del Centro Internazionale di Studi di Architettura A. Palladio,* Vicenza, X, pp. 65-78.

1968   A. VENTURA, "Considerazioni sull'agricoltura veneta e sull'accumulazione originaria del capitale," in *Studi Storici,* pp. 674-722.

1968   R. WITTKOWER, "Il balaustro rinascimentale e il Palladio," in *Bollettino del Centro Internazionale di Studi di Architettura A. Palladio,* Vicenza, X, pp. 332-346.

1968   W. WOLTERS, "Andrea Palladio e la decorazione dei suoi edifici," in *Bollettino del Centro Internazionale di Studi di Architettura A. Palladio,* Vicenza, X, pp. 255-267.

1968   G. G. ZORZI, "La interpretazione dei disegni palladiani," in *Bollettino del Centro Internazionale di Studi di Architettura A. Palladio,* Vicenza, X, pp. 97-111.

1968-1969   E. BATTISTI, "Proposte per una storia del concetto di Manierismo in architettura," in *Odeo Olimpico,* pp. 19-67.

1969   F. BARBIERI, "Le ville dello Scamozzi," in *Bollettino del Centro Internazionale di Studi di Architettura A. Palladio,* Vicenza, XI, pp. 222-230.

1969   P. BIEGANSKI, "I principii della composizione architettonica di ville palladiane come conseguenza della loro struttura," in *Bollettino del Centro Internazionale di Studi di Architettura A. Palladio,* Vicenza, XI, pp. 195-206.

1969   R. CEVESE, "Le ville di Andrea Palladio tra il 1550 e il 1560," in *Bollettino del Centro Internazionale di Studi di Architettura A. Palladio,* Vicenza, XI, pp. 163-173.

1969   N. DACOS, *La decouvert de la Domus Aurea et la formation des grotesques à la Renaissance,* London.

1969   E. FORSSMAN, "Del sito da eleggersi per le fabbriche di villa. Interpretazione di un testo palladiano," in *Bollettino del Centro Internazionale di Studi di Architettura A. Palladio,* Vicenza, XI, p. 149.

1969   P. FOSTER, "Lorenzo de Medici's Cascina at Poggio a Caia-

no," in *Mitteilungen des Kunsthistorischen Institutes in Florenz,* p. 47.

1969   C. L. FROMMEL, "La Villa Madama e la tipologia della villa romana nel Rinascimento," in *Bollettino del Centro Internazionale di Studi di Architettura A. Palladio,* Vicenza, XI, pp. 47-64.

1969   P. F. GRENDLER, *Critics of the Italian World: 1530-1560. Anton Francesco Doni, Nicola Franco et Ortensio Lando,* Madison-London.

1969   L. H. HEYDENREICH, "La villa: genesi e sviluppi fino al Palladio," in *Bollettino del Centro Internazionale di Studi di Architettura A. Palladio,* Vicenza, XI, pp. 11-22.

1969   C. LEWIS KOLB, "Portfolio for the Villa Priuli: dates, documents and designs," in *Bollettino del Centro Internazionale di Studi di Architettura A. Palladio,* Vicenza, XI, pp. 353-369.

1969   L. PADOAN URBAN, "Apparati scenografici nelle feste veneziane cinquecentesche," in *Arte Veneta,* pp. 145-155.

1969   A. PINELLI, "Palladio," in *Storia dell'Arte,* 1/2, pp. 175-179.

1969   L. PUPPI, "La villa Garzoni ora Carraretto a Pontecasale di Jacopo Sansovino," in *Bollettino del Centro Internazionale di Studi di Architettura A. Palladio,* Vicenza, XI, pp. 95-112.

1969   L. PUPPI (II), "Rassegna degli studi sulle ville venete (1952-1969)," in *L'Arte,* 7-8, pp. 215-226.

1969   G. SCHWEIKHART, "Studiem zum Werk des Giovanni Maria Falconetto," in *Bollettino del Museo Civico di Padova,* pp. 17-67.

1969   M. TAFURI, "Committenza e tipologia nelle ville palladiane," in *Bollettino del Centro Internazionale di Studi di Architettura A. Palladio,* Vicenza, XI, pp. 120-136.

1969   M. TAFURI (II), *Jacopo Sansovino e l'architettura del '500 a Venezia,* Padua.

1969   A. VENDITTI, *La loggia del Capitaniato,* Vicenza.

1969   A. VENTURA, "Aspetti storico-economici della villa veneta," in *Bollettino del Centro Internazionale di Studi di Architettura A. Palladio,* Vicenza, XI, pp. 65-77.

1969   S. WILINSKI, "La serliana," in *Bollettino del Centro Internazionale di Studi di Architettura A. Palladio,* Vicenza, XI, pp. 399-429.

1969   G. G. ZORZI, *Le ville e i teatri di Andrea Palladio,* Venice.

1969   G. G. ZORZI (II), "La datazione delle ville palladiane," in *Bollettino del Centro Internazionale di Studi di Architettura A. Palladio,* Vicenza, XI, pp. 137-162.

1970   F. BARBIERI, "Palladio in villa negli anni quaranta: da Loneo a Bagnolo," in *Arte Veneta,* pp. 53-80.

1970   E. BEVILACQUA, "La cartografia storica della Laguna di Venezia," in *AA.VV., Mostra storica della Laguna veneta,* Venice, pp. 141-146.

1970   A. CANOVA, *Ville del Polesine,* Rovigo.

1970   M. ROSCI, "Rassegna degli studi palladiani 1959-1969," in *L'Arte,* 10, pp. 114-124.

1971   E. BASSI, *Il Convento della Carità,* Vicenza.

1971   C. OSSOLA, *Autunno del Rinascimento. "Idea del Tempio" dell'arte nell'ultimo Cinquecento,* Florence.

1971   L. PUPPI, *Michele Sanmicheli architetto di Verona,* Padua.

INDEX OF NAMES AND PLACES

Proper names are in capitals; place names in italics. The numbers in bold type indicated the pages where the discussion is most fully treated. Abbreviations: a. = architect; c. = carpenter; e. = engineer; i. = illuminator; m. = mason; p. = painter; s. = sculptor; sw. = stoneworker.

FIGURES IN THE TEXT

PLATES

COLOR PLATES

SCALE DRAWINGS

PLATES

1 - Fratta Polesine: aerial view of Villa Badoer

2 - Villa Badoer: frontal view, from outside the enclosing wall

3 - Villa Badoer: frontal view of the main block, from outside the enclosing wall

4 - Villa Badoer: frontal view of the main block

5 - Villa Badoer: stairway and loggia of the main block

6 - Villa Badoer: the last flight of stairs and the colonnade of the loggia

7 - Villa Badoer: coffered ceiling of the loggia

8 - Villa Badoer: the Ionic colonnade of the loggia, seen from the inside

9 - Villa Badoer: the architrave and ceiling of the loggia, seen from the inside, from the north

10 - Villa Badoer: central section of the pediment, with the Mocenigo crest

11 - Villa Badoer: the inset of the right hand column of the loggia and the entablature above it

12 - Villa Badoer: the articulation of the main stairway

13 - Villa Badoer: the main stairway, seen from the north colonnade

14 - Villa Badoer: the basic complex by Palladio, seen from the extension of the south wing

15 - Villa Badoer: view of the main block with the north colonnade

16 - Villa Badoer: the south colonnade and its connection to the main block

17 - Villa Badoer: the north colonnade and its connection to the main block

18 - Villa Badoer: the north colonnade, seen from the interior

19 - Villa Badoer: the north colonnade, seen from the interior

20 - Villa Badoer: the trabeation of the south colonnade, seen from the interior

21 - Villa Badoer: the north colonnade

22 - Villa Badoer: the truss system of the north colonnade

23 - Villa Badoer: the ambulatory of the north colonnade

24 - Villa Badoer: the stairway leading from the main block to the north colonnade

25 - Villa Badoer: the same stairway seen from inside the colonnade

26 - Villa Badoer: the north wing, from above

27 - Villa Badoer: the south wing, from above

28 - Villa Badoer: the balustrade that connects the main block with the north wing

29 - Villa Badoer: the articulation of the stairway from the final landing to the north colonnade, seen from above

30 - Villa Badoer: the articulation of the major sequence of stairs, seen from above

31 - Villa Badoer: the last flight of the main stairway

32 - Villa Badoer: play of balustrades enclosing the final landing of the main stairway

33 - Villa Badoer: the balustrades that enframe the first two flights of the main stairway

34 - Villa Badoer: detail of the balustrade of the main stairway

35 - Villa Badoer: the south side

36 - Villa Badoer: rear view and north side

37 - Villa Badoer: rear view and south side showing terraced embankments

38 - Villa Badoer: the front enclosing wall, seen from the outside

39 - Villa Badoer: the rear enclosing wall

40 - Villa Badoer: the front enclosing wall, seen from the inside

41 - Villa Badoer: a segment of the enclosing wall in back

42 - Villa Badoer: fountain with a statue of Neptune

43 - Villa Badoer: fountain with a statue of Amphitrite (?)

44 - Villa Badoer: the portal leading from the loggia to the central hall on the main floor

45 - Villa Badoer: the central hall of the main floor with the fenestration
of the rear wall and the frescoes of Giallo Fiorentino

46 - Villa Badoer: the south wall of the central hall with the frescoes of Giallo Fiorentino

47 - Villa Badoer: the north wall of the central hall with tre frescoes of Giallo Fiorentino

48. - Villa Badoer: the large room on the left with frescoes by Giallo Fiorentino (southeast corner)

49 - Villa Badoer: the large room on the left with frescoes by Giallo Fiorentino

50 - Villa Badoer: southwest corner of the smaller room on the left with frescoes by Giallo Fiorentino

51 - Villa Badoer: view of the smaller room on the left with frescoes
by Giallo Fiorentino (east wall and adjoining corner)

52 - Villa Badoer: south wall of the large room on the right with frescoes by Giallo Fiorentino representing the Carrying Off of Ganymede and two gods in triumph

53 - Villa Badoer: view of the north wall of the large room on the right with the fresco of Leda and the Swan; and along the short interior wall, frescoes of the triumphs of the gods and mythological scenes by Giallo Fiorentino

54 - GIALLO FIORENTINO: fresco in the large room on the right. West wall with figures of Minerva and Pegasus

55 - GIALLO FIORENTINO: fresco in the large room on the right. West wall with figures of Venus and Pegasus

56 - Giallo Fiorentino: a grotesque on the east wall of the central hall

57 - GIALLO FIORENTINO: a grotesque on the north wall of the central hall

58 - GIALLO FIORENTINO: a grotesque on the north wall
of the central hall

59 - GIALLO FIORENTINO: a grotesque on the south wall
of the central hall

60 - GIALLO FIORENTINO: a grotesque on the south wall
of the central hall

61 - GIALLO FIORENTINO: a grotesque on the north wall
of the central hall

62 - GIALLO FIORENTINO: mythological scene (Diana, a river nymph, and Apollo?) on the south wall of the central hall

63 - GIALLO FIORENTINO: mythological scene (Diana and Satyr) on the north wall of the central hall

64 - GIALLO FIORENTINO: mythological scene (Diana, nymph, and a shepherd?) on the north wall of the central hall

65 - GIALLO FIORENTINO: two river gods (the Po and the Scortico?) on the south wall of the central hall

66 - Giallo Fiorentino: landscape on the west wall
of the large room on the left

67 - Giallo Fiorentino: landscape on the west wall
of the large room on the left

68 - Giallo Fiorentino: landscape on the east wall
of the large room on the left

69 - Giallo Fiorentino: landscape on the east wall
of the large room on the left

70 - GIALLO FIORENTINO: Bacchus (?); fresco on the south wall of the large room on the right

71 - GIALLO FIORENTINO: detail of the Carrying Off of Ganymede;
fresco on the south wall of the large room on the right

72 - GIALLO FIORENTINO: detail of a grotesque

73 - Giallo Fiorentino: detail of a grotesque

SCALE DRAWINGS

THE ARCHITECTURAL DRAWINGS WERE MADE BY PROF. ARCH. MARIO ZOCCONI AND BY DOTT. ARCH. ANDRZEJ PERESWIET-SOŁTAN, WITH THE ASSISTANCE OF DOTT. ARCH. EWA BORKOWSKA

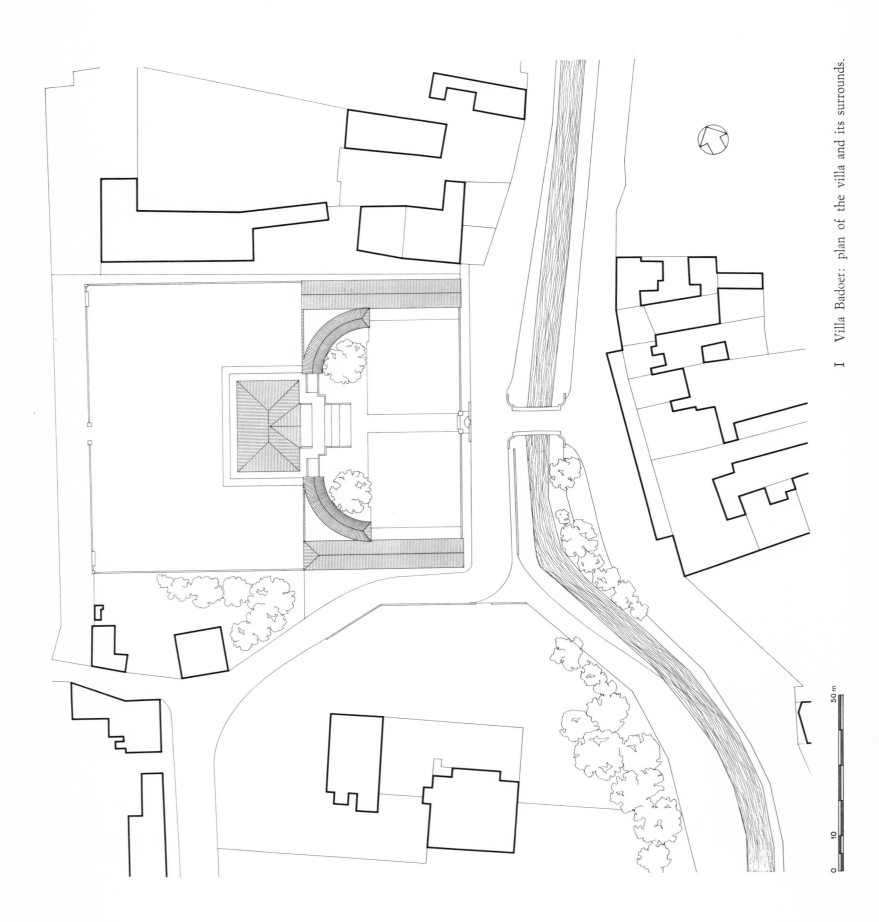

I Villa Badoer: plan of the villa and its surrounds.

0   10   50 m

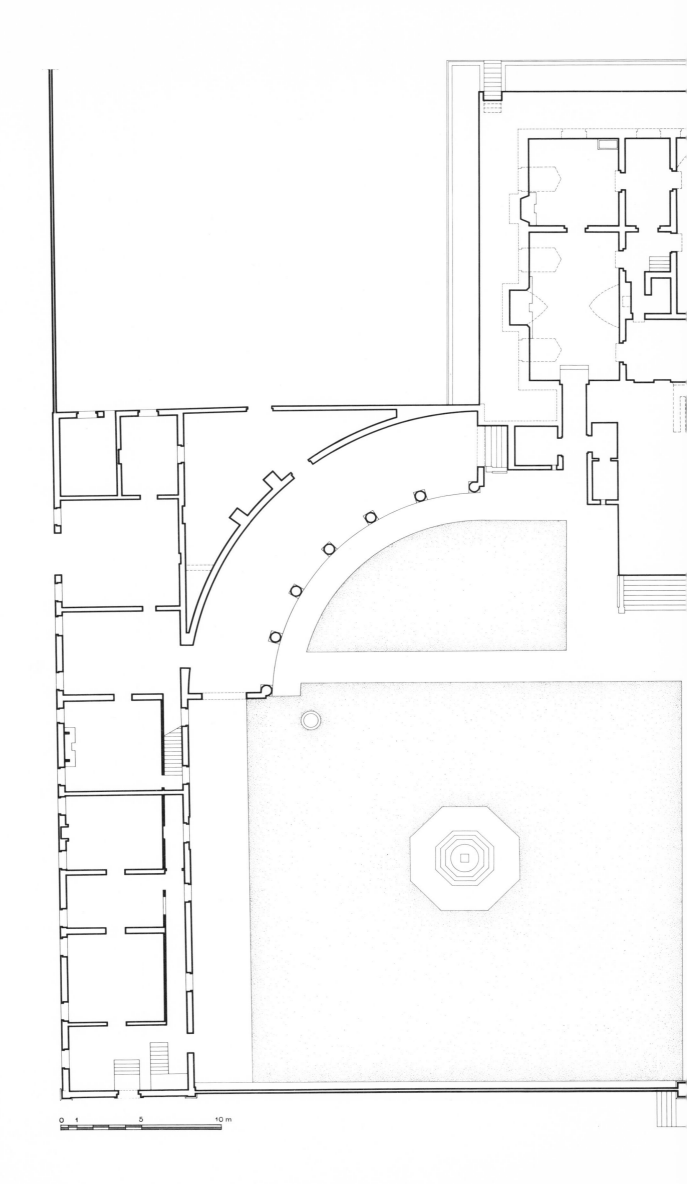

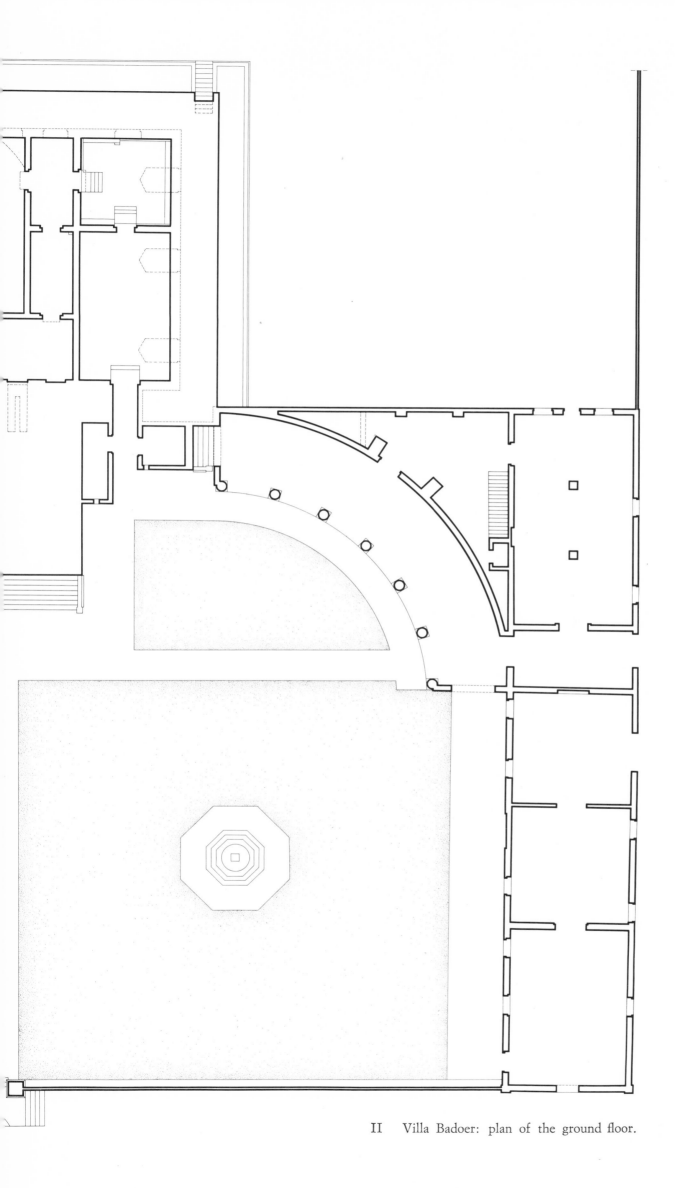

II   Villa Badoer: plan of the ground floor.

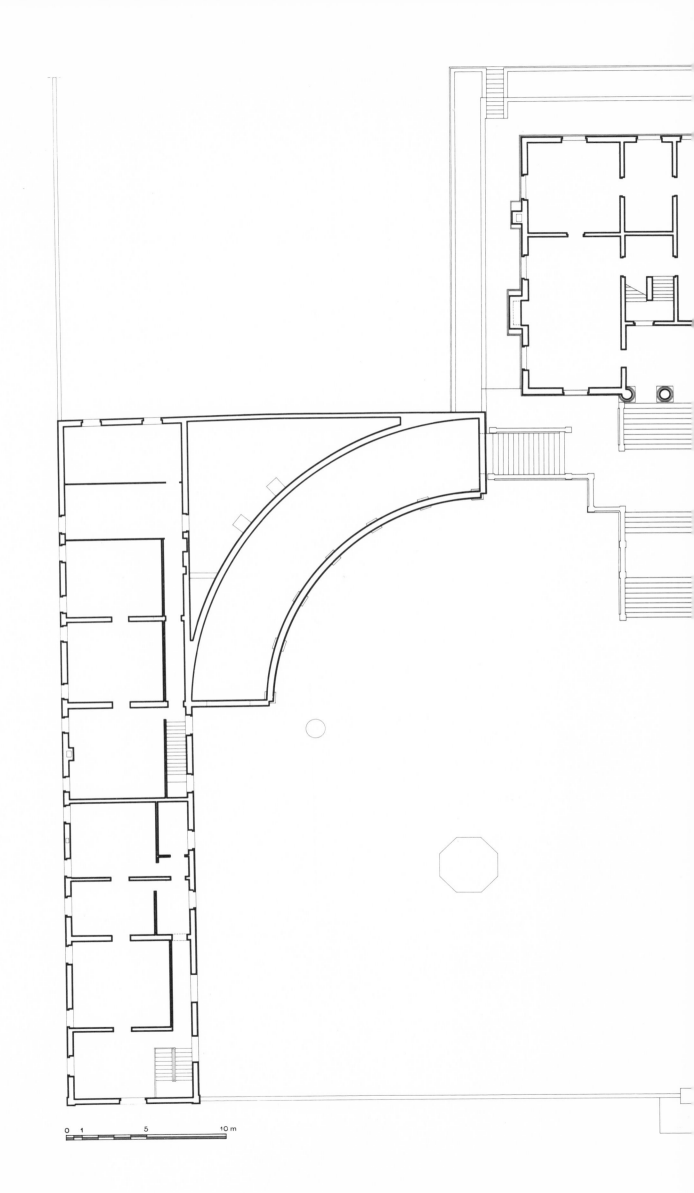

0 1   5   10 m

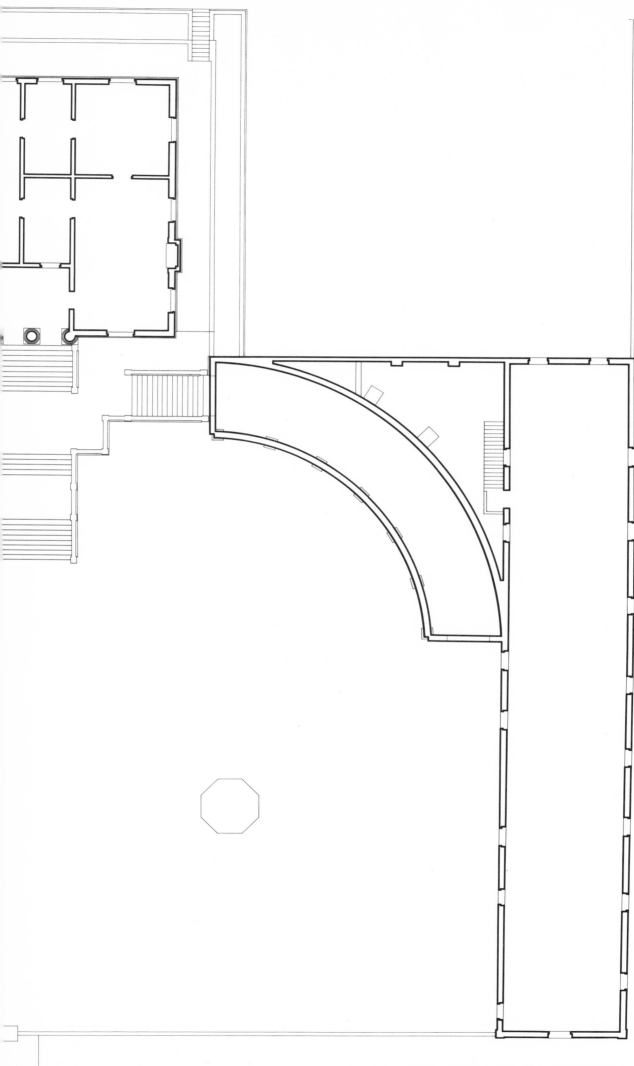

III   Villa Badoer: plan of the first floor.

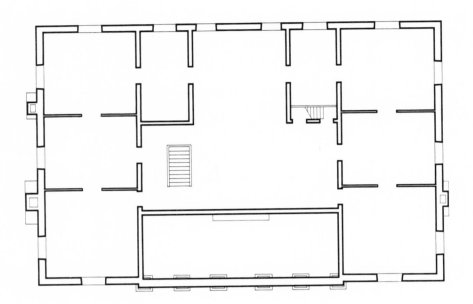

IV   Villa Badoer: plan of the attic.

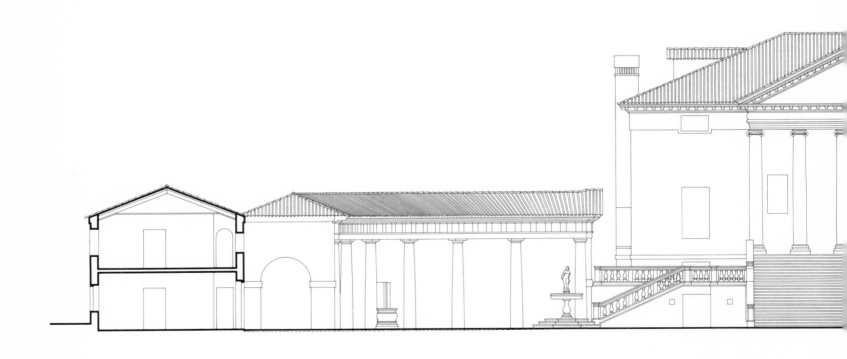

0 1   5   10 m

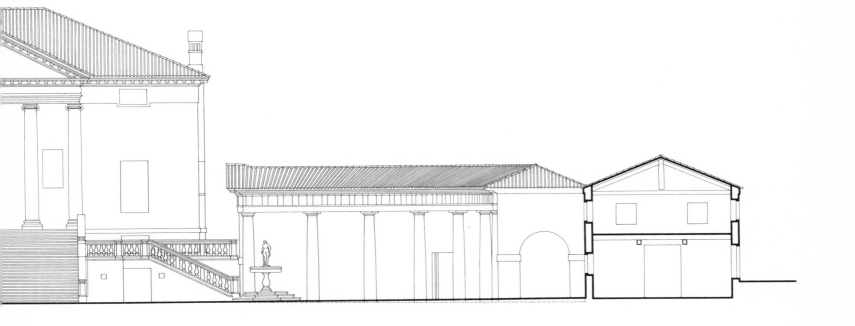

V   Villa Badoer: plan of the rear elevation.

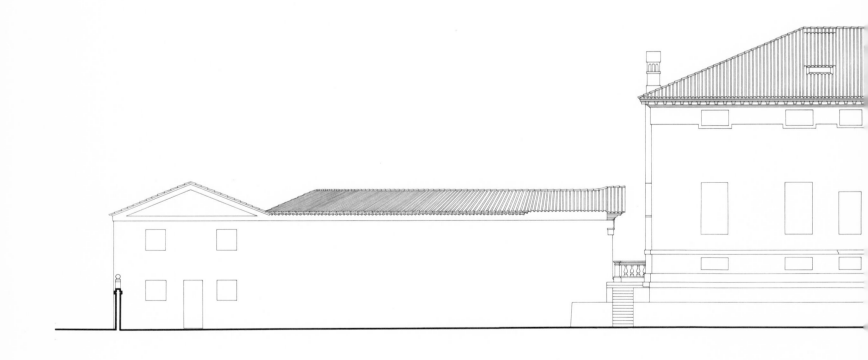

0   1   5   10 m

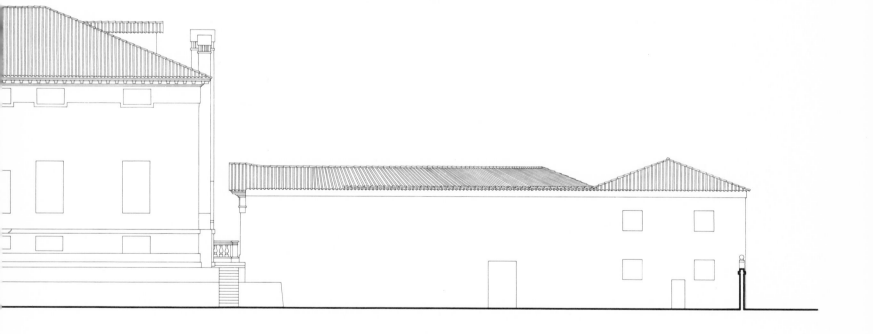

VI   Villa Badoer: front elevation.

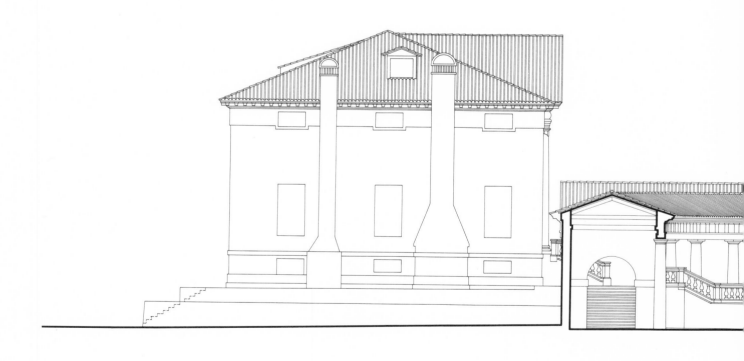

0 1   5   10 m

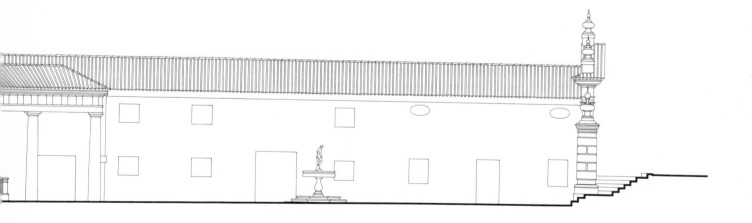

VII   Villa Badoer: cross section of the south colonnade and elevation of the north colonnade.

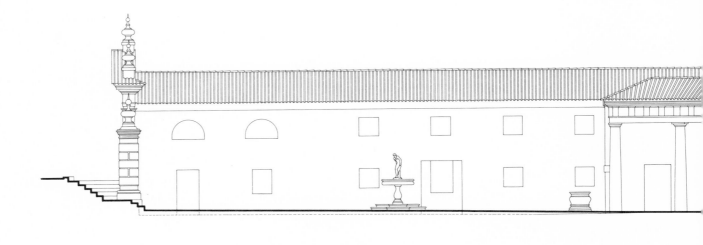

0 1   5   10 m

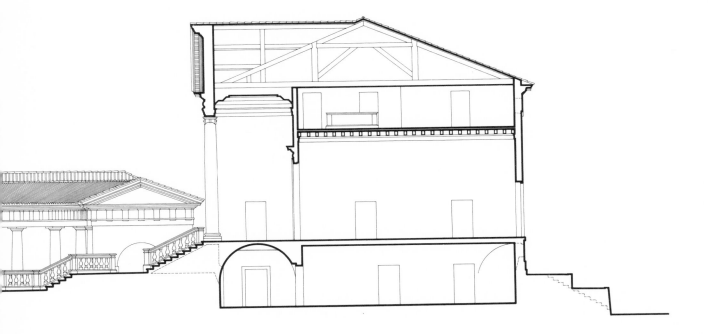

VIII   Villa Badoer: longitudinal section of the villa with elevation of the south colonnade.

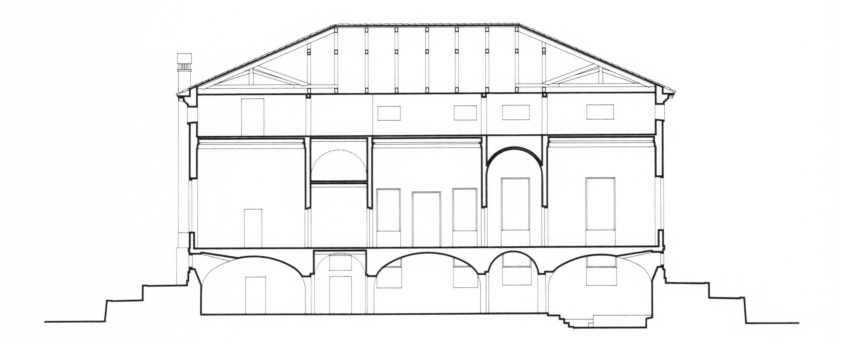

0 1   5   10 m

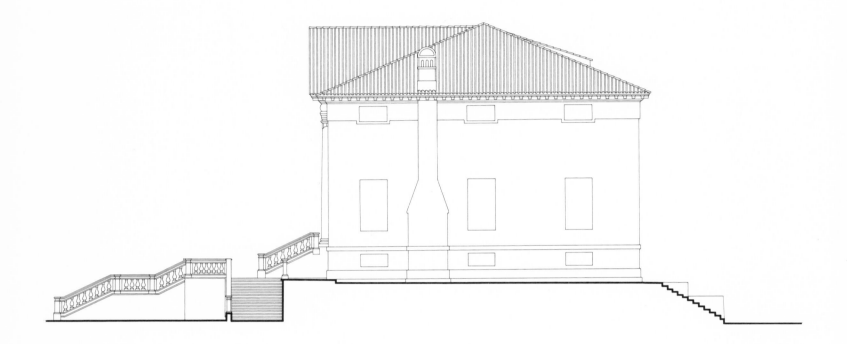

0 1   5   10 m

X   Villa Badoer: north elevation.

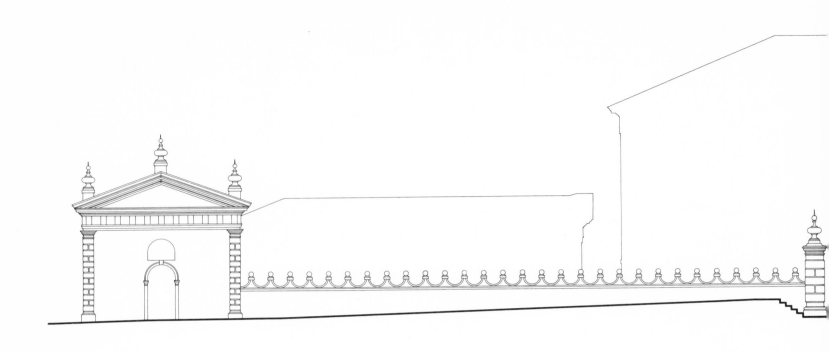

0 1   5   10 m

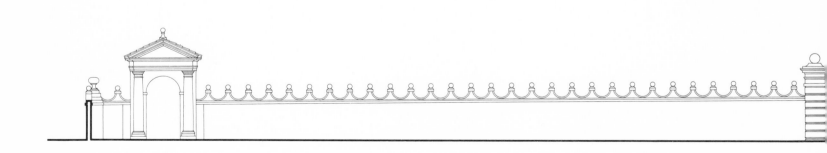

0 1   5   10 m

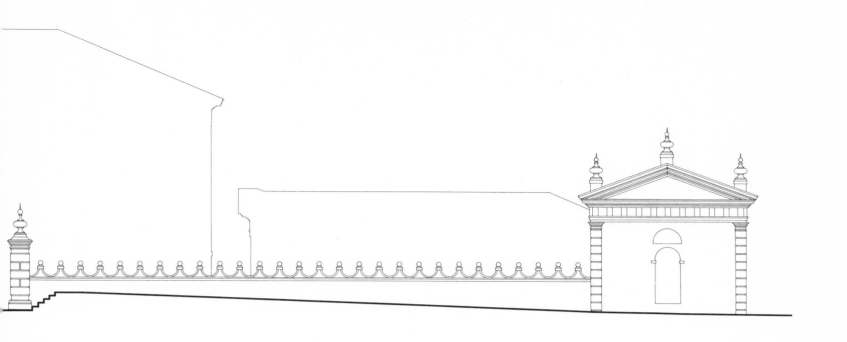

XI a Villa Badoer: elevation of the enclosing wall in front.

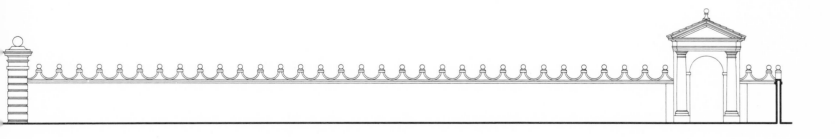

XI b Villa Badoer: elevation of the enclosing wall in back.

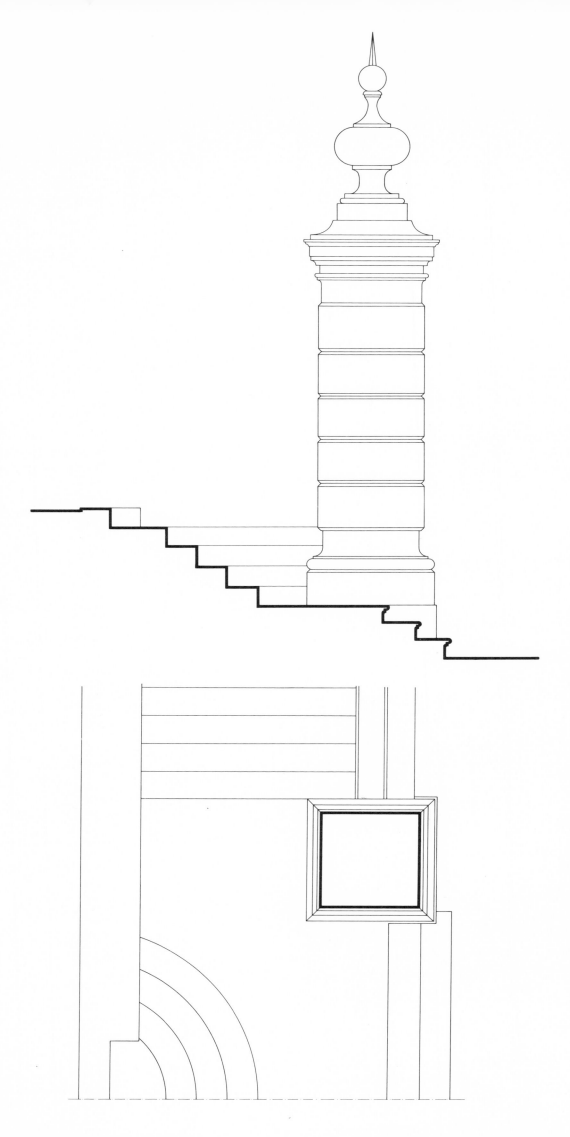

0   0,5   1   3 m

XII a Villa Badoer: detail of the main gate.

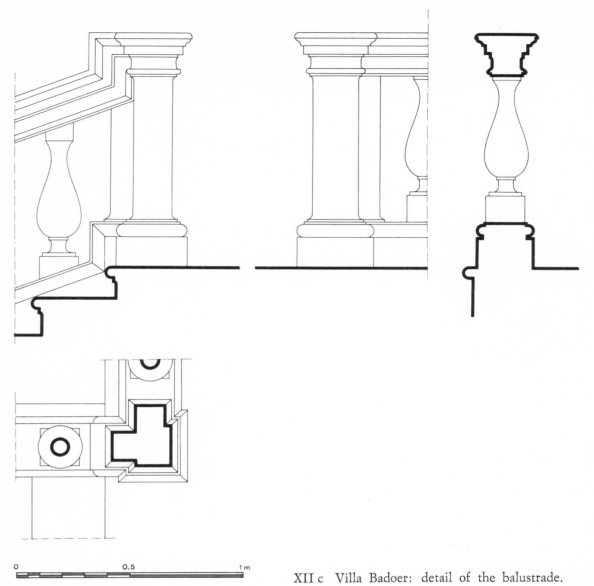

0   0,5   1 m

XII c Villa Badoer: detail of the balustrade.

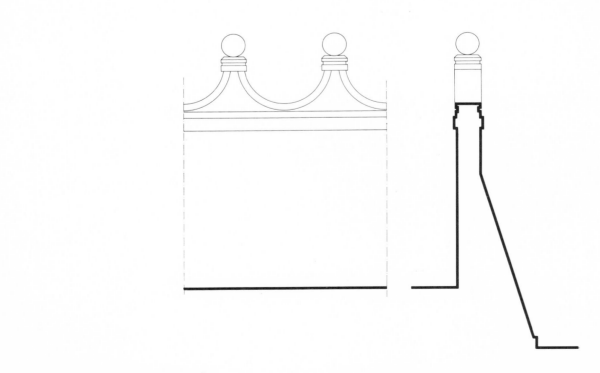

0   0,5   1   2 m

XII b Villa Badoer: detail of the enclosing wall.

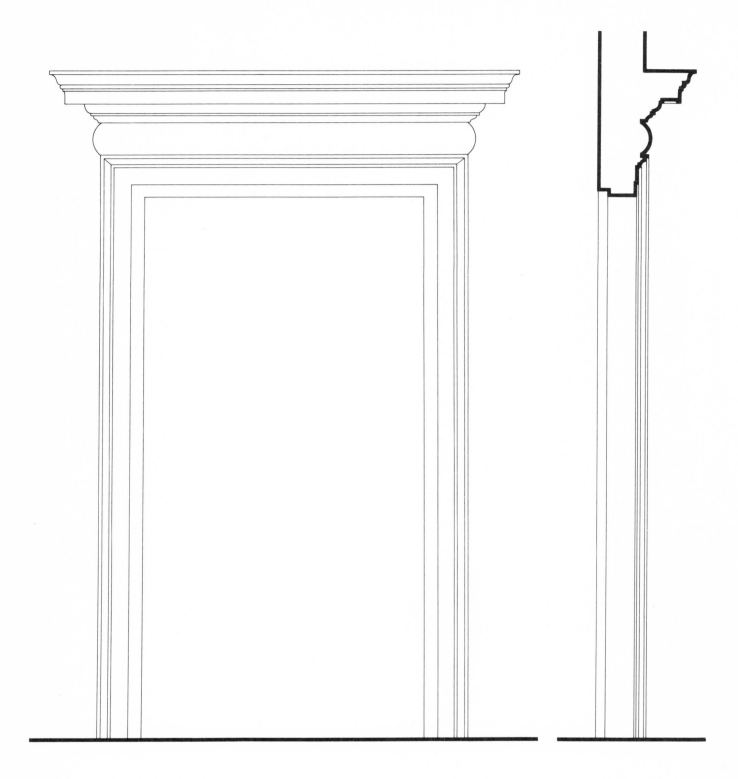

0   0,5   1   2 m

XIII a Villa Badoer: detail of the main doorway.

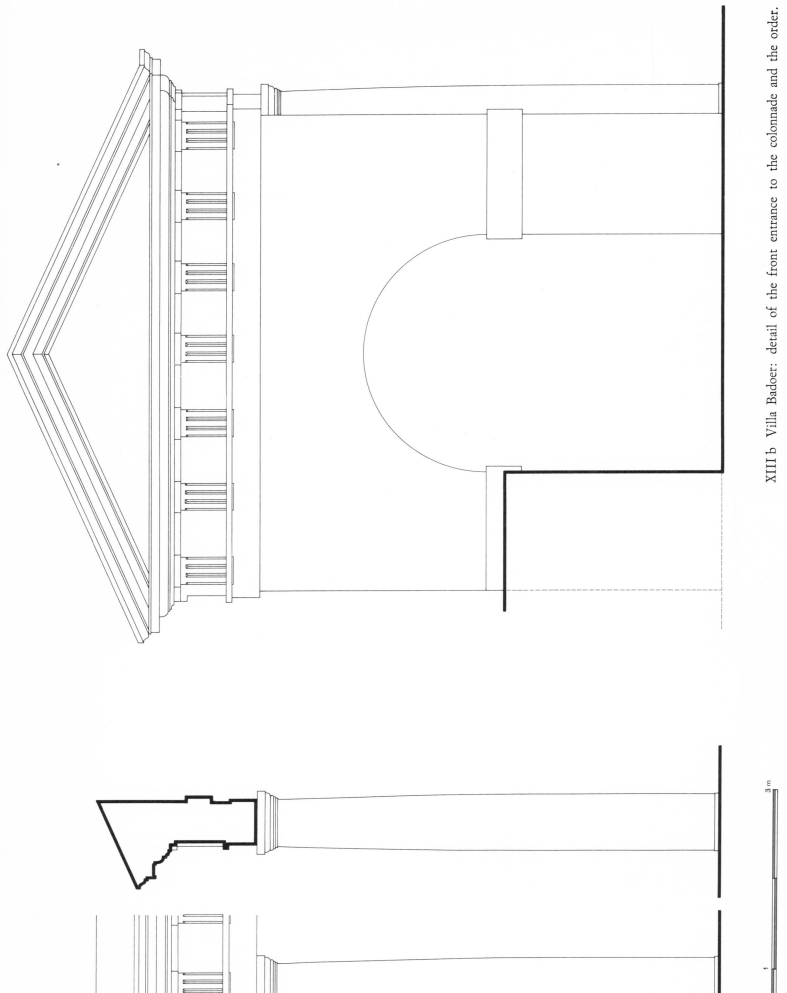

XIII b Villa Badoer: detail of the front entrance to the colonnade and the order.

0   0.5   1   3 m

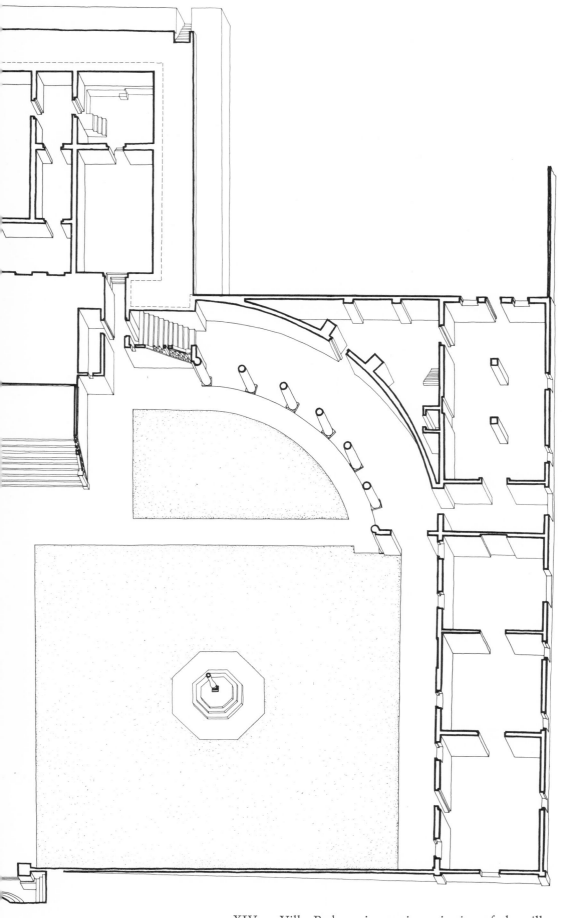

XIV   Villa Badoer: isometric projection of the villa.

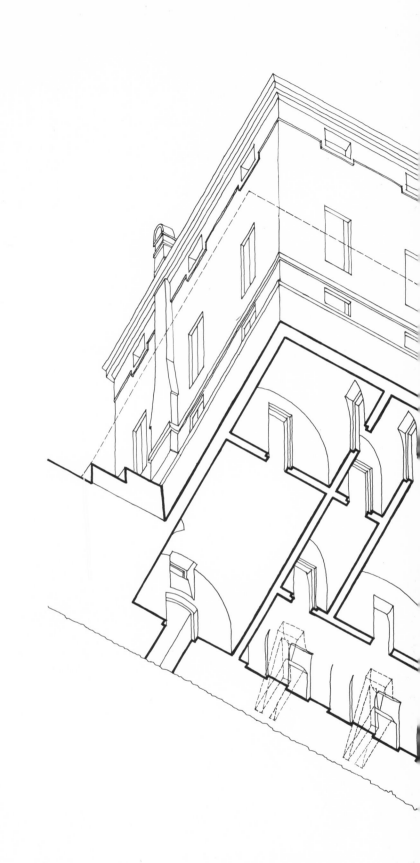

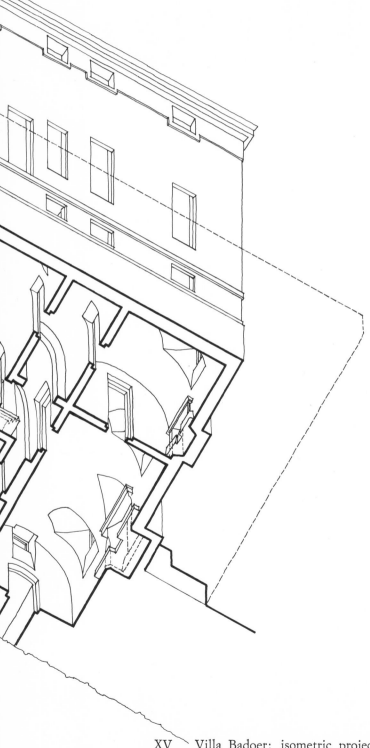

XV   Villa Badoer: isometric projection of the basement area.

THIS MONOGRAPH ON "THE VILLA BADOER AT FRATTA POLESINE" WAS PRINTED IN VICENZA BY OF-
FICINA TIPOGRAFICA VICENTINA GIROLAMO STOCCHIERO S.P.A. USING GARAMOND TYPE. THE PAPER
USED FOR THE TEXT IS PAPERALBA FROM THE VENTURA PAPERMILL; RUSTICUS, ALSO FROM VENTURA,
IS USED FOR THE SCALE DRAWINGS; AND FOR THE PLATES, LARIUS, FROM THE BURGO PAPERMILL. THE
BLACK-AND-WHITE AND COLOR PLATES WERE PRINTED FROM BLOCKS BY A. MONTICELLI IN PADUA.
THE DRAWINGS WERE REPRODUCED IN VICENZA BY FOTOTECNICA. THE BINDING WAS DONE AT THE
LEGATORIA INDUSTRIALE LAGHETTO E C. S.A.S. IN VICENZA.

DATE DUE